ABOUT THE AUTHOR

I was born on the Furness Peninsula and still live here on Walney Island, Barrow. The geography and geology of this karst landscape, together with the complications involved in teaching myself ways to move across it as a child with poor mobility, are central to much of my writing. Language too presents problems for me; how to find the words, how to say them out loud.

I work with artists from different disciplines; film-makers, theatre practitioners, designers, sound artists, curators, composers and musicians. My first collection, 'The Girl Who Forgets How to Walk' was published by Penned in the Margins in 2018. My poetry programme 'Earthbound,' was broadcast on BBC R4, and my prose poem/essay, 'Ways of Being' on R3.

I was short-listed for the Penguin Random House 2020 Write Now mentorship scheme and have received a Northern Writers Award for poetry. I'm currently writing a memoir, 'Breccia.'

FLOW
Kate Davis

VERVE
POETRY PRESS
BIRMINGHAM

PUBLISHED BY VERVE POETRY PRESS
https://vervepoetrypress.com
mail@vervepoetrypress.com

All rights reserved
© 2025 Kate Davis

The right of Kate Davis to be identified as author of this work has been asserted in accordance with section 77 of the Copyright, Designs and Patents Act 1988.

No part of this work may be reproduced, stored or transmitted in any form or by any means, graphic, electronic, recorded or mechanical, without the prior written permission of the publisher.

FIRST PUBLISHED JAN 2025

Printed and bound in the UK
by ImprintDigital, Exeter

ISBN: 978-1-913917-60-9

For my parents, who walked us over two hills to the beach every summer; my husband who taught me how to beach cast and long-line and how to stay safe in the sand-swallowing tides of Morecambe Bay and for our children and grandchildren who take to the water with us and swim with seals.

CONTENTS

Rain	11
Ice	39
Fog	75
Cloud	123
Steam	151
Mist	177

FLOW

a verse novel

Rain

Rain, stinging rain, skelped in from the west
when the child first appeared on their finger of land.

Though her body was bitten and bruised,
hollowed with hunger, she stumbled on up the hill,
her legs hardly able hold her up.
She could smell the strangers creeping closer,
hear their ugly, urgent word-sounds –
she floundered forward – they followed her.

A sudden cliff. She sank to her knees,
stared at gray water that sprawled forever –
nothing made sense – its hiss and sigh
was the metal-stink of squirming piglets
when the sows were farrowing – sky and air
were water – the soil she stood on was water –
her body and her thoughts were water –
everything angry
                    agitated
                                  gray.

She wanted to pray but the only word
she could say was *uischa* – couldn't stop saying it,
uischa uischa – shouting it now,

her reedy voice vanishing in rain –
she turned to the watchers, whispered, *uischa*.

She was frightened by their fierce faces,
the men reaching out to touch her hair,
their sour reek and strange sounds,
the way they copied her word, like starlings –
uischa   uischa –
       A woman unpinned
the child's cloak, snatched at the wet wool.
She clutched her sodden clothes around her,
tried to stand, sure they were going to
hurl her into the heaving water.

She tried to pray but water was making
her thoughts into a mass of mad insects
swarming in her skull

       open your mouth don't leave me eat the food I found for you
       open your lying mouth eat it eat the food don't leave me don't
       leave me open your mouth don't leave me eat it

       no prayer came.
She let go of the cloak, let it fall,
scrabbled at the strange red soil,
dug her nails deeper down,
clawed out clods of earth, threw them
at the crowd crushing in around her.
A boy with a broken tooth took hold
of her raised arm – someone held her
by the shoulders, tried to stop
her frantic gouging at the ground –
flecks of spittle flew at her from
their immense mouths as they moved in,
  jaws   working   working   working

making no noise – nothing right –
light squeezed – sound gone –
whatever small strength she had – gone –
she saw her hand stretch into blackness
that was death   sleep   night-dark fruit.

The prayer words came then, terrible and true,
she could hear her mother speak them,
watched them weave the air, felt them
fly like arrows to her brain and belly.
She gathered them all up in her gullet,
spat them at the jabbering strangers,
bared her teeth, began to snarl –
rain ran in her mouth, she spat
that too, heard herself howl.
A dog growled. Then they grabbed her.

*

The hill people never harmed the girl
and though her tongue was not their tongue
she started to learn some of their language,
knew the tribe called themselves
Hegantii – people of the hill,
knew their greetings, their words for *light*
and *food*. Often, they asked of her father,
asked of her grandfather, her people, her home,
asked her name, she never answered,
her heart and head too full with words
she had to keep safe – her mother's words.

Because she never shared her name
they called her *Uischa* – her word for water.

As she had no liking for life
behind the wooden walls and banks
circling their village on the cliff,
they left her bowls of barley-meal
by the brackish pools behind the dunes.
When they collected crabs in the channel
between their island and the main-land
they took her with them, taught her the laws
of water and tide, of moon and wind
so she would stay safe in a dangerous world.
When she wandered too far, they followed –
when she walked into the waves,
eyes fixed firmly on the horizon,
swam out towards the lump of land
that sometimes appeared on the skyline
in a certain light, they called to her,
told of terrible things that lived there –
haunting, hungry horrible things.
Uischa felt their fear for her
in the words she knew and the words she didn't,
felt a fear of that place fix itself
like a maggot in her mind.
Yet the salt sea beguiled her, drew her in,
held her high in its gray waves

>*it's a kind of consolation*
>
>*it's all I have   this balance between world*
>
>*and water*
>
>*it's holding on   being held   it's the rise   the fall*
>*the peak   the trough   the lift and hold*
>*the salt   the cold*
>*the grit   the sand   the slap and sting*

    the churn   *the roll*
    the push   *and pull*
    the heave   *the tow*
    the lift   *the hold*

    the salt   *the cold*

it's

    the salt   *the salt*   *the salt*

    and the cold

*

There was talk in the tribe of the thing she had hidden,
some said it was cold and still, like the dune pools
when the wind dropped and they saw their own faces
staring up from the surface. And hard – made of a metal
that smelled like iron, though it couldn't be iron
as it stole any face that looked into it –
they were terrified it would take their spirits too.
Some swore it was bright with blood-red enamel
or glancing turquoise like the gannet's eye.
Some spoke of shapes engraved on its back,
three perfect circles and in them more circles
like maps of the journeys made by the stars.

That day, when the child came to them
and they carried her back, limbs bound, still screaming
her unknowable words, they knew the thing
had power, the child had power – she should be
its keeper. When she finally stopped fighting
and slept, the chief covered it in cloth
and tucked it back inside her tunic.

She had come – it had come –
the tribe could never change those things.

*

Winters were vicious – often the villagers
feared she'd frozen, searched till they found her.
They'd try to coax her to come with them
to the warmth of their round huts for a while.
But there was some small, dying thing
inside her – a moth thing looking for light,
feeble wings fluttering for want of it –
she couldn't save it, couldn't let it go.
They didn't know what had happened to her
though they knew that flittering, fragile creatures
could come to live in a sorrowing child
whose grief has nowhere else to go,
so they left milk and lengths of their thick
woven cloth to warm her and asked
nothing. There was comfort in their care
and she prayed for them, helped at harvest,
gave warning when predators crept close to their cattle.
When they went to the mainland to mine red earth
for iron, she worked with the women, weaving
or cutting wood for the charcoal clamps.

Still, she didn't talk to the tribe,
though often she went to the grove of oaks
as the sun slipped into the western sea.
There she prayed and sang her words
softly into salt-sharp air,
aching for anything that could tease
threads of memory – home – her mother –
that face she thought she knew but couldn't
quite remember. There were times, at twilight

as she sang among the trees,
the voice she heard was not her voice,
it came from far away and with it
was something she could almost catch –
something like a stream in summer,
easy as a froth of flowers –
ransoms, dog-rose, gentle daisies –
something like the scent of skin.

These were the moments the moth thing settled,
the times that tethered her to this island –
a strip of clay, a spit of stones
hunkering down in wild, wild winds.

Although she always prayed alone
the hill-folk followed, listened to her,
let Uischa's unknown language leach
from the girl's tongue into their thoughts.

*

As the years turned the life she'd lived
with her own people began to wither,
while certain memories stayed pin sharp.
These she nurtured to keep them safe –
reliving all the dreadful details
of those last days before she left
when her world was dying, was a price worth paying

> *barley has blackened   rotted away*
> *in cold relentless rain*
> *my mother can't get up from her bed*
> *we're starving*
> *children die first for want of food*

*the sickness is getting worse those who can
scavenge for anything to be found
most of the men are too weak to hunt
so they trap what animals there are
bring them back
we will eat any slimy crawling creature the famished can't afford
to feel disgust
each night we lie down
too hungry and too scared for sleep...*

*yesterday my mother gave me hers said she wasn't hungry
her skin hung loose starvation soured her breath
I knew she was lying
still I ate it*

*this morning I left before first light walked
as far as I dared from home
scoured every bush for fruit we might have missed
tore hazel twigs to grab the last nut carried them carefully back
I held the berries out to her she wouldn't take them
I shouted she said she didn't want them
told me I should eat them myself
I tried to make her forced berries in her mouth
dark dark fruit
I was pushing it in smearing it over her mouth she tried to turn away
her body humped and she vomited a thin thread that hung quivering
from her chin I couldn't I couldn't I couldn't
stop myself screaming at her eat it
eat the food I picked for you eat it eat it eat it eat it*

*she touched my cheek and cried quietly
I wiped the mess and mucous from her face
lifted her shoulders
felt the shock of bird-thin bones through her tunic
the blood tubes in her neck twitched like the pigs' when they see the*

sharpened blade
her heart was stumbling   I thought of my own when I'm running
with the rest of the children   how it hammered in my chest
like rain on rock
her heart was a wounded animal
skittering   halting   racing from hunters closing in for the kill
I sang to her   made up silliness
I think we slept...

a strange thing is starting to happen
mother is kneeling   washing me as if
I'm fragile as a flower   her lips move   shape words
no sound comes
she rocks her body so that the rocking
the washing the word-shapes are all one
her eyes are closed   I close mine
and I am mired in the middle of something
slipping towards a dim place   scrabbling
away from the edge where earth un-melds
I am afraid
small flames flicker
in the fireplace   I squeeze her arm
she stirs   turns to me and the world settles
its stillness is dangerous

my mother's shaking shadow-hand
curves round my cheek   she says – Give me your hand girl
 I do
a slick of cold shocks my finger-tips
I pull away   press my eyes shut
she tells me to open them
I obey

and there it is
the cold thing

glinting in firelight

it holds a face
mother
no
but it looks like her   I try to touch the face   icy fingers stop mine
I squeal and she smiles holds the thing close we're in it
the same
but not the same   I kiss her other mouth
she says a word – Mirror
I don't know the word   the thing
I don't know how it got here to our home   what it wants
I think it is stealing her strength to make itself strong

she turns it to show me its spiraling patterns
its bird-bright   flower-bright   colours
tells me to tuck it inside my tunic
I don't want it there but I think of her stuttering heart and do as she says

she sleeps

I wake to the sound of some animal scratting
outside our door
I don't understand
why is it there   where's the pig boy

then I remember the rain   the sickness
bodies bloating where they lie
no-one to take them to the place of the dead

I lean towards my mother and touch her
she's colder than winter rain   colder
than the mirror she made me keep
I hold her   kiss her hair   her hands
tell her about the fruit we'll find

when she wakes   sweet sun-warmed bullaces
blackberries fat with juice

I don't know how long we've laid here   night and day have dissolved
there is only now
and my mother next to me

thirst forces me to my feet
the water carrier is empty
my cloak hangs on the hook
I lift it down
pin it on and open the door

I can't see her face from here
I try to force my eyes to focus but the space is a forest
tears grow fat as I try to remember my mother's face
already it's blurred

my mother's voice
there's only silence

my mother's touch

my mother   O my mother

then the walk

*

By Samhain of the sixth year
Uischa was small but quick and strong
and lish as any willow wand.
Still she chose to live out in the open –
water was like coming home,

she was safe in the sea where air fizzed
from her limbs when she dived and darted,
like the herring who spill their silver lives
through swaying waves. Her old life was waning,
but the sacred words were alive inside her.

That harvest was good – grain pits full –
the tribe gathered, gave offerings to gods
at the oak grove. Uischa went with them,
her sung words and soft-breathed chants
had woven themselves into their world.

On the final day of the festival
a horrible thing happened to her

> *I'm at the North end of the island*
> *in the dunes   it's getting dark*
> *an odd cloud sweeps over the bay*
> *very low from the north*
> *I watch it come close to the shore*
> *its shape is so solid that I can outline its edge with a finger-tip*
> *it looks like a great gray bird skimming in to land*
> *the cloud sinks*
> *swallows the sand-dunes*
> *swallows me   and I am lost in darkness*
> *grabbing at marram grass   trying to run   but the cloud*
> *catches me*
> *drags me back*
> *its weight presses my throat my thighs*
> *so terrible*
> *so heavy*
> *I can't fight can't breathe can't breathe can't breathe*
> *when I stagger I'm held by my hair I hear the sea's long moan*
> *somewhere close a seal is crying*
> *I try to say my mother's words*

they gibber on my tongue   gag me

*

Heat-dull cattle milled in the mud
of the dune pools the day the babies were born.

Their mother kissed two quivering mouths,
whispered the words she kept in her head –
each thing three times, each time their eyes
opened wide, watched the movement of her lips.

Their faces were the same but not the same,
then exactly the same, then the boy was a stranger
and the girl was her grandfather, or he might her mother
laughing in her lap but she didn't know her daughter.

Uischa stared as they sucked and wriggled,
searched in the mirror for her own mother's face.
Their flickering breath, their skin on her skin,
came from a far place faded in rain.

whatever had happened inside her body,
that made these two things rip their way out
in a shriek of pain, had shocked Uischa –
her face was filled with it, eyes stared
like a startled deer. Yet she seemed to know
what to do with them. The villagers watched,
brought her cloth to keep them warm,
brought broth when she was weak from their birth,
brought her herbs to heal the tear
the twins made as the tore their path from her.

Slowly, slowly the shock faded
and Uischa began to love them both,

laughed at their antics, blew bee-kisses
into fat little necks, spoke softly in
her mother-tongue to soothe them. Some nights
she cried at the sound of their quiet breath.

She had no names for them so the Hegantii
called the boy Brendhan, his sister Brigha.

*

The twins were not like the village children,
they were ponderous, silent, slow on their feet.
They'd appear at a distance, heads tilted together,
their beautiful blank faces always watching.
The two little figures would stand face to face
mimicking how the hill-peoples' mouths
moved when they spoke, how their bodies
undulated and swayed when they walked.

Earth made Brendhan and Brigha heavy –
water made the pair of them perfect.

When the villagers went out in their boats
Uischa and the twins would bob way ahead,
the children chittering and calling, or drifting
far below, limbs trailing like tentacles,
hair flowing and swirling as they swam.

Though the two seemed strange to the tribe
they let their youngsters talk with them,
teach them their Hegantii words,
show them how to shape red clay
or whittle wood into animals and people.
They told the twins the story of
the before times, when the tribe lived in

the Great World, caught fish, found fruit, grew grain
and everything in the World was good –
how the island was made when a man –
a man too vain, too proud to ask
the sea spirits for their blessing before
he took fish from them, too greedy to offer
a gift to the sea for its generosity –
this man angered the sea so often
the sea spirits cleaved a chasm and made
the village an island cut off by a channel
too deep, too wild for people to cross.
The sea spirits saw the tribe's suffering,
felt pity for them, said if they were patient,
if they waited a thousand winters,
they'd wash in one pebble or handful of sand
with every tide, to join the island
back to the world. So they waited and waited
a thousand winters and slowly the sea
grew less angry until two times every day
the spirits allowed them walk across
back to the land – back to the world.

*

The twins grew very fond of the villagers –
when the children were sad or scared
they sang their mother's sacred songs
to console and comfort them.

Uischa heard them – she hadn't sought
to share her rituals with the tribe but they
seemed to take strength from them and she
couldn't stand to snatch that away.

The three caught fish or foraged for food,

when they found none the tribe fed them
and in return they would find fish –
lead the boats to schools of bass
and the darting shoals of silver herring,
dive for flatties, lift lobster and crab
from beneath rocks on the sea bed,
throw their catch in the little craft.

Uischa showed Brendhan and Brigha the mirror –
they touched the circles but neither couldn't bear
to look at the face it stole if they held it.
She taught them the words she learned from her mother,
said them must hold them safe in their hearts.

When they asked why they were not
like the other children, or asked about family,
Uischa told the twins the truth –
that she was a child when she came to the island,
she'd walked a long way – she didn't remember
much of her home, that her memories were
like a clay cooking pot dropped on a hearth –
on one piece she was a girl planting grain,
on others, her mother hands made bread
or pushed her dark hair under a pin.
When they asked what her mother looked like
she said the fragments didn't hold a face –
when they asked of the walk, she tried to remember

>*it's confusing   a few things from before are clear*
>*but the journey is just a pattern of land*
>*in my mind I see shapes*
>*dots of juniper   patches of pine*
>*circles of elm on open ground*
>*dips and hollows   dark with different shades of green and brown*
>*the ground was a picture and I had become a bird*

watching myself walk by night
cower in any small space I could find
if I thought there were people nearby

I remember the terror

I remember the rain

I remember what I was forced to call food   *no-one*
should eat such filthy things

I think I recall the time I got here
better than the journey
though now it's hard to say
what parts are a story I've told myself
what are memories
what are scraps of some long-ago dream...

spikes of marsh grass have given way
to reeds reaching far above me
only the swaying of their seed-heads
in the wind helps point the way

peaty soil has become sticky mud
that seems to want to swallow me
everything here   even the air
is new   it's not just the smell of it
the new thing has crept into my chest
it makes me dizzy for a moment

birch twigs thrash in an astounding wind
and bare blackthorn stiffens against it

through branches I see sky   still gray
yet different   I see it spread

unfold
like slow petals over me   opening itself wide
as if it wanted   to show me
its most precious secrets
it's so huge it scares me to death

what daylight there was is dimming
when I lug my exhausted limbs
from the ooze and stumble out onto
the banks of a river where rounded rocks
edge what should have been water

but no water flows

birds with curved beaks
poke in shallow pools
they watch me   I try to work out
why water would vanish
when rain has fallen for many months
I'm too tired to think
I sit on the stones
put my feet in a little pool
black snails scurry about below the surface
one crawls over my foot
I shudder
but I don't have strength to shake it off

rain runs down my legs   still the mud sticks
the smell of it is like nothing   like something
it makes me think of my mother's cold face

and this new sky   the way it seemed to unravel above me
before I lost sight of it in the reed beds
it must have been a trick of the light

I look up

and there it is   too wide   too high
another sky   another world
I don't know it and I'm afraid

on the river bank
a crow tugs silently at a scrap of fur and flesh
I don't have the strength to fight for it

the pool is deepening
water flooding in fast from the south
making small whorls   dividing round rocks

the stony bed is a sudden stream
the river is returning
I don't understand

fear forces me to my feet
the pool is already part of a pattern
of rapidly rising rivulets   behind me is the bog
I can't go back
the opposite bank is steep   bushes
grow here and there   could I grab one
I race over rock and silt to the stream   step in
before blind panic can stop me
the strength of the water is shocking   it thrusts itself against me
like an animal
I wade up to my waist
then my chest
eyes fixed on one bush
force my feet to keep going forward
force my eyes to focus on that bush
to look at its single sodden leaf
to see myself holding it in my hand

finally I feel my fingers close
on a branch and I know the river won't take me

its terrible grip eases
until I'm sliding on the steep bank
snatching at the bush and sobbing

when I wake it's dark   I'm shivering
my whole body shudders   won't stop   I try not to think
just lie by the bush
wait for light

at last it comes
I see the river is flowing fast now   but the water
is running the wrong way
what horrible monsters might there be in such a place
I shut my eyes   and slowly
slowly
I am warm
so warm   sleep is coming back   spreading through me
warming   soothing saying let go   let go
and I'm letting go
sinking into sleep where there's no cold
no pain
and my mother is
my mother is

something sharp is sticking in my ribs
waking me   taking away my warmth
pulling me back to that blighted place
I push it away   it stabs again
keeps stabbing   someone groans
then sleep is gone and I cry tears
of disappointment as I drag
myself to sit up

at my side
is a chunk of bread   dark and coarse
like the bread me and mother made
when I pick it up it's wet
but it smells like bread   I eat it
and wait

My tunic is twisted   I wriggle
it back round   that's when I realise
the mirror – her mirror – is missing

I must have dropped it
did I drop it
I glance round dead winter grass
but I already know my mirror has gone
I'm so shaky I can hardly stand
have to haul myself up on hands and knees –
I have lost the last thing she gave me
and I'm too feeble to go back for it –

I climb   soon the bank is so covered with trees
I can't see which way to go   I follow the incline
pray that my gods gave me the bread   not some beast
that wants me fat enough to eat

trees are thinning when I smell smoke

someone's lit a fire   I can't stop
thinking of the thing that made it
and what it wants to do with me...

the last things I remember of that time
are shadows   watchers in the wood
feet creeping close   the cliff
gray rolling water

barking dogs
a boy with a broken tooth
the taste of blood

*

Years notched by. The twins, now taller
than Uischa, were always together.
Sometimes they'd stare at the sea for days,
sitting silently side by side
on the cliff. If the villagers coaxed them
to come away, they'd look confused,
shake their heads solemnly, turn back to the sea.

When months of rain ravaged the land
Uischa smelled the bloated stench
of rot, knew again the keen of a terror
that waited, open-mouthed, saw over and over
in the gape of its gullet, her small hand lifting
a cloak that hung on a hook by a door.

In the village sickness spread,
people sweated and coughed – bright blood
frothed their lips. Those who didn't die
were too weak and hungry to tend crops
or to fish. Uischa watched the twins
for signs they were struck down too
but all three stayed well. They caught whiting,
shrimps, picked seaweeds and leaves,
brought them back to the village.
Only a few could eat the food.

The villagers clung to Uischa's clothes,
begged her to get her gods to spare
their children, offered up their own spirits

if Uischa could save their children from death.

Each day Uischa prayed for the people,
murmuring the words as she worked,
urging the twins to say them with her.
Nothing they did stopped the deaths –
the boy who carved animals for Brendhan,
the woman who plaited Brigha's hair –
the baby Brigha sang to – all dead.

They laid their corpses with the others.

Uischa kept going. When Brigha and Brendhan
couldn't carry on she was frantic – furious –
dragged them towards the oak-grove, said
they must all pray harder, only prayer
could save the villagers. All three were almost
dead on their feet, still she hauled them
towards the trees

> *we chant   Brendhan and me but Brigha*
>
> *stands silent*
>
> *I wait   whisper – Speak Brigha –*
> *she shakes her head – Speak daughter –*
> *she looks away*
>
> *Oh God*
>
> *she looks away*
>
> *when I turn her face to mine I feel*
>
> *the sacred words wither*

world falters

patterns unravel   paths roll backwards

the words are dead

I can't speak   I don't know what to do

I look to the oak trees

hear only rain

Every day Brendhan and Brigha
carried more corpses to the place of the dead.
Uischa's silence shocked the tribe,
they pleaded with her to pray for them,
cried out for her help. She turned away
from their gaunt faces. It was Brigha who spoke –
she told them the land was no longer good,
prayer couldn't change that – said she would
build them a boat to sail from the sickness
if they had the courage to come with her.

They were bewildered. Again, Brigha told them
Uischa's words would not save them.
A few people whimpered, someone shouted
for Uischa to tell them what to do.
Uischa stooped, picked up an acorn,
saw it was soaked and starting to rot,
let it fall from her fingers, turned away.

*

Brigha began building.
                        Uischa and Brendhan

did as she asked, worked without stopping
till oak and ash then ox-hides became
a vessel bigger than any the villagers
had ever seen. They were scared of the way
it flinched with every seventh wave,
as if its heart was still in the hills
and it longed for the gladdening green of land.
They knew it grieved for its own great roots
twisting down, tethering it
against crashing winds, knew it still craved
the dark silence of soil and stone.

Uischa climbed in, held out her hands
to the trembling people. They never moved.
Brigha and Brendhan kneeled by the boat,
bent their backs to make a living step
that would take the villagers' weight.

For three days and nights they stooped
as rain soaked the living, the dying, the dead,
until even fear was washed from them.
A woman wept as she handed her son
up to Uischa. Slowly they came.
At sunset on the third day the twins
felt the last pair of feet lifted in.

A gibbous moon glowed as Uischa
slipped, like a spirit, onto the shore,
walked to the dunes – the place where
she'd first felt safe, where food for them
was left by the tribe, where she'd huddled from winds
that never let up, laid in marram grass
while salt and water dried on her skin
and the sounds of the sea soothed her to sleep.

The dune pools shone black. The place
the three of them had made their home
looked as if they'd left long ago –
already forgetting them, sinking in sand.

A clay pot the hill-folk brought food in
lay on its side. She picked it up,
carried it carefully into the pool.
In her head her mother's words
were trying to arrange themselves,
but her thoughts wouldn't stop whispering

> *O water   O still water of dune pools   frog-spawn*
> *striped snail   damsel fly*
> *blue shimmer of sea holly in summer*
> *O song of high-flying geese   nights of moon and no moon*
> *O limpet   peeler crab   crawling winkle*
> *swimming shoals of silver bass*
> *O tide   O lugworm whorling sand*
> *razor clam*
> *rockling and sandsker*
> *O smell of metal and sheep*
> *sweet hazel-nut and berry and barley-meal*
> *O mice and perfect pebbles   O holy oak trees*
> *O breath of babies on my neck   my sweet warm babies*
> *O diving seals   O you wind   you wild tides of winter*
> *island   my island*
> *I am leaving*

When the water was up to her waist
Uischa let the bowl fill to the brim,
watched it tilt, slip into dark water.

*

Sometimes, at top tide, the wind will drop away –
sea hang suspended, neither ebb nor flow
but quiet – water holding its breath,
its heart-beat slowing before the turn.
So it was on the day they set sail –
they waited to feel the familiar drag,
sensed it seconds before it happened.
Breeze lifted – Uischa watched colour leach
from land as it floated backwards – black
fading to violet   to gray   then gone.

Ice

North –
    the new boat nosed its way,
    quietly at first, finding out how to flex
and straighten with the waves, learning
for itself how deep water worked.

The faint hump of land the hill-people feared
sank with the sun and was lost to sight.

Seals bobbed beside the boat,
summer shoals circled and children stretched
over the side to see the huge ovals –
leatherbacks feasting on jelly-fish.

They went west and passed, too close,
a finger of land like the one they'd left.
Some wanted to stay but Brigha said,
We have to go further from the sickness,
somewhere the stink of so much death
can't follow us – we have to cross
to the other side of the great gray sea.

She knew it to be true, knew too
that even though dread haunted her,

tied knots in her trembling gut
so she thought she was going to be sick,
a part of her she couldn't control
wanted to go and keep on going,
to see where water and tide would take them.

When wind dropped the few who were well
tried to row. The tiny boats
the hill people fished from proved to be
poor preparation and progress was slow.
All those not sick took their turn,
strained aching backs and breaking arms
until air became breeze, breeze became wind
and the sail swelled back into life.

As days passed the hill-people found
their bodies and minds slowly became
merged with the measure of water so that
the vast void of ocean was less terrifying.
They gave themselves over to the boat – to Brigha

> *all our lives we've watched the villagers*
> *make their way to mother's rituals*
> *her words and chanting were warp and weft*
> *of the cloak that kept them warm*
> *Brendhan and me had both repeated*
> *the sacred ceremonies since we could speak*
> *each thing our mother taught us*
> *was a cord that kept us tethered close*
> *to the earth   so tight that sometimes*
> *I could barely breathe   I was heavy*
> *with the weight and the worry of it*
> *I told Brendan*
> *he knew before I spoke*

when sickness came again they cried out
clutched at the cob-web of my mother's words
she and Brendhan began
I couldn't
she said – Speak – Speak daughter –

I couldn't

she looked for a long time into my face

then some lit thing faded from hers

*

Brendhan listened when Brigha asked
for help to read the signs, choose a route –
when he answered her, his voice
was a new voice, stronger now,
though Brigha sensed he was still scared too.

They count the nights of the moon's momentum,
watch the stars arcing above them,
wait for changes in the wind's strength,
the sea's mood.
            You'll know which way
we need to go, he said. She nodded
but Brigha's brain was bursting, as if
squabbling magpies, scolding her loudly,
were stopping her from thinking straight

> *my head can hardly hold it all*
> *I talk to Brendhan till I think I know*
> *which way we should steer   sometimes the sick*
> *cry – Uischa   help us – she'll pray*
> *but she can no longer lose herself*

in the words

she looks so small

I've done this to her with my disobedience

*

Veering north, the villagers grew stronger,
the world grew weirder. Their fragile boat
was quick to learn what the sea was saying,
what the air was thinking. Islands appeared –
if they put ashore the villagers asked Uischa
to make the land safe before they'd step on it

> *the hill-people always kept mother from harm*
> *when they're scared she can't see them suffer*
> *so she says the dead words to soothe them*
> *it's odd   we're the ones with nothing to help us*
> *yet they hold on*
> *the old words are broken*
> *but they still believe*

> *I've talked to Brendhan   told him I can't help seeing this boat*
> *as a heap of ash branches and scraps of skin*
> *and when I fall asleep the bits fly apart*
> *pegs   lathes   mast   sail   people   us*
> *spinning silently through the air*
> *further and further away from each other*
> *I didn't tell him*
> *that mother's face is the last thing to fade*
> *and in the dream   she's always crying*

Rain turned to sleet as they stepped onto
a jagged spear of rock jutting out

of the waves, it's top very white and compelling.
The pinnacle spun above them. No-one spoke.
The sea breathed gently. Soon Brigha sensed
a new thing, tilted her head to the west

> *it isn't a sound   not quite   not yet*
>
> *the air is disturbed   the weight of sky*
> *is changing as well   its watery darks*
> *are specked white with countless slow particles*
> *the specks become circles and in them more circles*
> *and the sound is an ocean I've never laid eyes on*
> *till above us the world is filled with white birds*
> *spiraling down so their wings brush our faces*
> *and the blue of their eyes looks into our eyes*
> *the children are laughing   trying to touch them*
> *holding out hands for the white birds to land on*
> *but the birds are already circling higher*
> *catching the air that carries them away*
> *the children are climbing up the steep crags*
> *lifting the long mottled eggs from high ledges*
> *carrying them carefully back to the boat*

*

As seasons slid by, the sun's yellows
seeped from each dawn till all that was left
was a liquid kind of light. On still days
it settled on everything, silver and thin.

When the weather was bad the sea swallowed
every bright scrap into its iron belly.

It was colder than Brigha could have imagined.
Each time they came close to new land

the people pleaded, *Is this the place?*

I don't know   I don't know   I don't know
I'm afraid to stop and afraid to go on
but we have no choice
wind and currents say I've left it too late to turn back

what if I'm wrong
what if we could still turn round
what if we've passed the place where we could be safe
what if I'm taking all of them
to their death

something makes me want to keep moving
it's like an insect irritating my thoughts
telling my selfish greedy heart to keep pushing them north

I don't blame them for being scared but
they babble and beg till my head feels
as if it'll burst
when they wait   watching me like sheep
it's all I can do to stop myself yelling – Leave me alone –
they're eating me
bit by bit
chewing off little chunks   before long
there'll be nothing of me
but bones

when I look at my mother she looks away
though I've done a terrible thing I thought she'd forgive me
instead she punishes me
I need her and she turns her back
I will not ask for her help again

*

A small island swelled into sight,
its surface smooth as if worked and polished
to a gleaming mound of gray rock.
Nothing grew there but the villagers needed
to feel the good earth under their feet
so Brigha told them to beach the boat
high and safe on the hump of land.
They turned to Uischa – she did what they wanted,
then they climbed ashore, shivering and scared.

When they'd walked off their stiffness and aches
Brigha told them to get back in the boat
but the place was so peaceful they begged to stay
for one night, to know what it was
to be safe on the land, to be still.

Darkness fell – each dreamed the same dream –
the island was moving – not bobbing like the boat,
its surface was lifting ever so slightly
then sinking back – resting and rising –
they felt themselves anchored, curled together
in some warm, remembered sea.

They were still asleep when the strange island
turned north, rose higher and headed off.

They slept through seven nights and days.
When the island stopped, they woke to a new
blackness.
            The air was different to anything
they'd known before – as if it were brittle,
might shatter if they shouted. Night was no canopy
curving above them – more than cold,
it was bright needles piercing brain and body,
crackling deep in their chests when they breathed.

Uischa ushered them back in the boat

   we wait

   as light sparks in the east
   the island sinks silently and we float free
   on a sea as smooth as the mirror my mother
   keeps secret
   the whole world is faltering
   path-ways unrolling   all things uncertain

   when the ball of sun breasts the horizon
   the island appears again close by the boat
   looms right beside us not making a ripple

   then   as if earth has finally forgotten how such things
   should happen
   fine rain surges up into the air with a sound like a sigh
   and droplets fall around us as bright specks of ice

   a great eye appears in the gray of the island
   its iris a map of the places it's journeyed
   it's pupil a circle of stones in the darkness

   soundlessly   slowly

   the living eye blinks

   and I feel the eye of the world closing with it

   when it opens the heart of the world opens for me

   and blooms like a flower out of pity and love

it's leaving us

pouring its brilliant body back into the sea

slipping away

*its fabulous tail draws a perfect curve
and it slides under the surface out of sight*

*

Columns of ice taller than the cliffs
of home winked and glittered whitely,
sparked with spears of sudden colour.
Where the surface of the sea should be,
great frozen chunks jostled and creak
muttering horribly under the hull.
Thick cloud covered the sun –
the terrifying pillars towered above them
as ice thumped against thin leather.

The villagers waited for Brigha to tell them
what they should do. She stared at her mother's
bent head, bit her bottom lip hard,
tasted blood, but Uischa didn't
turn to her daughter, didn't look up.

Brigha tried to recall the star-tracks
and moon-patterns, work out wind's intentions
but her thoughts were seeds blown from thistles,
she was too weak and weary to hold them

*my brain aches for the weight of waves
to squeeze out all the villagers' voices
for silence and blue space to take me where water and salt*

will blister my lips
grit scour me cleaner than I've ever been
then   maybe
I might sink into mud
become mud
so the heft and moil
of their awful need can no longer reach me

*

She turned her face up so they wouldn't see –
a flock of geese flew far above,
so high that the arrow-head of their flight
could fit onto the tip of her fore-finger.
She pointed to the sea-path that mirrored
the bird's sky-path. Brendhan changed course.

They sailed on through shrinking days –
air stank like some febrile, fetid thing,
burned terror into their throats, filled
their minds with all manner of mad
ravenous, sharp-nailed creatures, crawling
towards them from a flaming pit.

Land at last – frozen mountains loomed
spitting fire and yellow fumes –
the pit-creatures flinging fiery rocks.

Wind dropped to nothing as night lengthened.
They trembled with horror and cold, then hunger
overwhelmed them and they went ashore

> *they're so desperate but they don't ask*
> *for any comfort the old words could bring*

> *I've brought them to this   taken even*
> *that scrap from them   better they'd died of the sickness in their*
> *hill-top huts*
> *than to face what lives in this frozen land*
> *this is my fault*
> *their trust in me is ridiculous*

They found food of sorts on the island of ice,
trapped the fat birds with bright beaks
that nested in the ground. Nothing was normal –
the sea was solid – days were shrinking,
disappearing – light disobeyed the laws
they knew – colour flooded and flickered,
sending green spirals across the dark sky
as if the world was breathing out slowly,
watching its breath float in frozen air.

Then there was nothing – only night.

There was no comfort now for Brigha
but her brother Brendhan near her –
through that winter when the world
was silenced by the falling snow
Brendhan held his trembling sister,
heard the whisper of the snow-world,
smelt the heat of Brigha's body,
which was a new kind of creature,
which was shaking, clinging, saying,
Close your eyes my brother Brendhan –
though even then she was alone.

*

No-one died – or they were all dead –
Brigha couldn't tell. Time was a carrion crow

measuring the ground. Gradually sun-light
warmed the world, ice groaned loose
around the boat, bones and sinews
started to thaw. They left that place.
Days lengthened – it had been a long time
since Brigha stopped counting, but Brendhan still did.
The boat held its voyagers safe in its hull
as, time after time, fog engulfed everything,
soaked everything. They sailed on
to whatever waited for them all.

*

The ball of late sun was balancing on
the edge of the earth – light was low,
shadows sharp, everything etched
like lines drawn in damp sand –
when Brigha thought she saw something
low and heavy on the horizon,
but her body and brain were broken –
she curled herself close to Brendhan and slept.

For the first time since they sailed
she dreamed the hill and the dunes they'd left –
stood in the oak-grove – sat on the shore –
saw a huge bird over-head,
so big its shadow blocked out the sun –
saw her mother hold out the mirror –
saw its pattern of three perfect circles,
glittering bright with blood-red enamel,
glancing turquoise like the gannet's eye –
watched her mother mouth the old words –
saw the mirror swallow the oak-grove –
saw herself slowly falling forward
into some frightful, frozen place.

Brendhan was waking her, shaking her shoulder.
The boat was close to a narrow beach –
trees grew darkly down to the water,
all alike, bristling towards them,
ranked like warriors spearing the sky.

The hull grated on the gravelly shore
of another land. They waited, listened –
sun hauled the long shadow of trees
back to their roots, held them briefly,
then tilted them towards the east.

Dusk.
      Fear forced Brigha's nails
into her palms like a punishment.
She screwed her eyes shut and stood shaking
at the prow pretending to watch
the forest for some sort of sign

    their need is burning into my back

    I am so small

    the trees are taller than the cliffs we left
    and too close
    their sharp sappy breath scares me
    perhaps I've brought us to a place
    filled with sickness or slicked with the blood
    and flesh of other feeble travelers
    torn by the teeth of terrible beasts   *what if the water*
    is tainted with poison
    filled with foul slimy...

    Brendhan slips past me   *steps from the prow*
    the sound of his feet on the stony beach

is like mother's lips on my forehead

*I hear him say – Open your eyes sister –
but I only think of horrors hidden
in the black woods where no birds sing
he takes my hand   unfolds my fingers
places a pebble   asks – What do you see –
I see a smooth gray stone   I see
the shores of home*

*they are hiding their eyes   burying heads in hands
I tell them they must look at me   at the pebble
tell them this land might be like
the hill-top home they had to leave
my voice is thin   I know they don't trust me
they tremble in the bottom of the boat*

someone cries out – Uischa   save us –

*she doesn't answer
she turns away
anger scalds   surely she'll help when they beg her
when I'm helpless
when I have nothing at all to give them*

Night. Darker, more dangerous, than nights
on the open ocean, cloaked everything.
Brigha could hear them in the blackness
muttering Uischa's meaningless words,
comforting each other with empty chants –
the sound of it crawled across her skin,
her scalp, burrowed into her brain
until she heard herself shriek –
*Shut up! She won't help! Her words
won't save you. If you don't want to die*

shut up and do as I say. At day-break
Brendhan and me will go ashore
to see what manner of land we've come to.
While we're gone you will not ask
Uischa to pray. If we came back unhurt –
our limbs unbroken, minds unchanged
by any creature or spirit that calls
this land their own – then you will know
her words are false, you must forget them,
they have no power to protect you.

Rain was falling when Brendhan and Brigha
told the tribe to stay near the boat,
to eat only things they knew to be safe,
then waded through waves to the narrow beach.

The forest gloom seemed a solid thing –
a wall to keep them out. They walked
along the shore line, looking and listening –
birds sang – something huge
soared far above without a sound –
a creature crashed through trees close by
making guttural, snorting sounds
then seemed to stop. They froze in fear,
waited for it to fly from cover
and attack.
             No creature came.
A tiny movement of twigs made them
hold their breath, until a burst
of belligerent chattering broke the quiet
and two furry bodies, both small and gray,
bundled from the forest, squabbling ferociously.
Squirrels – the twins knew them at once
though they were too big, their coats the wrong colour.
The big one chased the smaller squirrel

into the lapping waves where it
squealed and spluttered indignantly.
Brigha laughed at the animals' antics –
seeing creatures that looked like those
she knew from home made her less afraid.

The twins walked from forest to wetland,
heath to rocky outcrops, where water
tumbled in torrents down hill-sides,
big cats tensed their beautiful bodies
preparing to pounce and the yowls of wolf packs
hung in the night air. They trapped birds
and burrowing things when they could
but hunger always hovered close.
Though berries hung in luscious bunches
they didn't know them so daren't eat.

For three days they searched for signs
of other people – the smell of smoke,
a path, a hut, a patch of grain,
any sound more human than animal –
now and then Brendhan thought
he heard a new bird call or caught
a hint of a shape flickering through the forest,
then a deer would break cover or a bird take flight.

When they got back to the beach they could tell
something was wrong before they reached
the boat – nobody appeared or answered
the call the twins had always used
to let the villagers know they were near.

The boat was deserted. They started searching
for signs– found footprints, a snapped twig
and flattened grass, followed it until

they heard voices they knew – the villagers
were close by.
                In a small clearing
the tribe huddled round a ragged heap –
a child curled on the ground, her skin
blotched purple, body twitching.
Her father tried to hold her still
her mother sat on her haunches, too shocked
to move. Slowly the jerking stopped
and the child appeared to fall asleep –
her thin arms fell, flaccid at her side,
her face relaxed. Brigha ran forward,
shook the girl, slapped her hard,
slapped her again, she never stirred.

A great wail went up from the tribe.
Brigha told them to be quiet,
laid her head on the child's chest
and listened for a long time.
At last, as if from far away,
she sensed a faint pulse, slowing further
with each fragile beat. *What happened?*
she asked. A hand stretched out, showed her
the glistening fruit the girl had eaten.
Brigha slapped the berries to the ground.

One by one the tribe began
to chant the words Uischa taught them.
Although she understood their anguish
Brigha told them to stop at once. Brendhan
hauled the girl's shoulders higher
and Brigha forced her fingers between
blue lips, hoiked out bits of the berries
then pushed further – there was no response –
Again, Brendhan said. She tried

once more to make the girl vomit,
to purge her of the poisonous fruit
but the little body was lifeless. Brendhan
laid her on the gently on the grass.

When her mother's wail of grief
tore away the terrible silence
the tribe keened – not the words
Uischa had bought with her – they
sang of loss in their own language –
someone's sounds and words of sorrow
taken up tremulously by the rest,
voices rising to rhythm, then chant,
only to falter and fall away.

The girl's sister started to sing,
quiet notes quivering on the air –
not her own tongue – she sang
Uischa's song. Someone began
to ululate – raw, unfettered sounds
as they gave themselves over to their grief.

From the forest figures edged forward –
men with weapons and warrior faces
crept unseen towards them. Uischa
was first to sense that they were there.
She turned to them, gave a sudden cry.
Brigha stood up when she saw strangers
with sharp blades surrounding them –
the death songs stopped. A man put down
his spear, stepped towards Brigha,
both his open hands held to her,
the bright berries the girl had eaten
in one. He spat – threw them away.
In the other a ball of bark

and leaf chewed to pulp. He put
the mess into his mouth, pointed
at the child. Brigha couldn't breathe.
The strangers came closer, weapons ready
to strike. Brigha took a step back.
When the man bent over the body,
the girl's father hurled himself forward
to shield his child but he was so scrawny
the stranger held him off with ease.
Brendhan wrapped his arms around
the sobbing man until he stilled.

The stranger spat out dark saliva
into his palm, examined it closely,
dipped his first finger in it and
began to rub it into the girl's gums,
repeating the action, again and again,
massaging the mess under her tongue,
behind her teeth, his gaze moving
from face to chest and back.
                              When finally
he stopped the girl was still as death,
the livid purple patterning already
beginning to fade. He moved the body,
curling the child on her left side –
they knew it instantly – the grave position –
then he began to back away.
His tribe tensed, ready to protect him.

As if they were all one single animal
the strangers faded – shadow to forest –
then nothing until the sound of retching
broke the silence.

*

It rained and rained. Sometimes they saw
a trace of the people who lived in that place –
smelled smoke when the wind blew from the West –
came across faint tracks – caught sight of figures
darting soundless – shadows through trees.
When they did well at the hunt, they wove
baskets from grass, left gifts of meat
for them.

    The land they'd come to
was cool – cloud often covered the sun
and moon for many days. But buds
were open, birds built nests – they saw
the world had woken from winter,
and summer warmth would follow soon.

Although they'd neither animals nor crops
spring meant renewal and rebirth.
The land was like home – it wasn't home
but they saw things like those they'd left –
pebbles, birches, pine trees, birds,
rocks, grass, insects, rivers –
and at night a moon and stars moved,
circled the sky in ways they knew
and ways that left them wondering.

For the first time since they set sail
the tribe had hope – the child survived,
the gods had sent someone to save her –
there was food to be found – summer would come –
perhaps there was time to plant the precious
seed they'd brought?

        Though Brigha urged them
to clear land, sow seed, search for clay

and ore-bearing rock, build round-houses
and dig grain pits, the exhausted people
wanted to rest and observe their rituals
of Beltane. They ignored Brigha,
went into the woods to find honey for beer.
They gathered what grains they knew to be good
for food, began to brew bowls of beer.
Sprigs of blossom were picked by young people,
animals were hunted for the feast.

Uischa kept her distance, hid
away at the edge of the encampment.
All day she quietly continued collecting
material for the houses the hill-folk
would need when the weather worsened.
Days passed – Brigha and Brendhan
prepared soil, planted seeds.
Though Brigha begged and berated them,
they took no notice.
                        On the third night
the tribal elders took Uischa
by the arm, tried to lead her
to their fires. She shook her head
but they lifted her high, bore her aloft
singing the songs she had sung to them,
praising the power of her words
giving thanks to her for saving them.

They set her down, circled her,
dancing, chanting, drinking beer.
Their din disturbed Brigha from
her weary sleep. To her, the sound
meant danger – some malevolent thing
attacking. She shook Brendhan awake,
ran towards the noise not knowing

what she would do, only that she had
to protect the tribe. In the light from fires
she saw Uischa standing, surrounded
by unsteady villagers, their drinking vessels
slopping beer as they laughed loudly

> *I remember the sound*
> *their stupid slurred singing*
> *mother standing in the centre*
> *someone was whispering in my head*
> *saying I must*
> *make*
> *her*
> *leave*
> *send her far from*
> *force her from*
> *make her   send her   saying I must*
>
> *force her far from make her*
>
> *– Stop –*
>
> make them stop
>
> help me Brendhan
>
> make them
>
> make them make
>
> I didn't ask
>
> for any of this I tried to   help me brother   they were dying
>
> I didn't ask   this is my fault

make her

make

her

make   her   for

make   her

for

make

her

for-

give

me

*　　　　　　　　＊*

The tribe were stunned, stood silent as Brigha
made her mother leave. They tried
to find Uischa, called to her,
searched each day till darkness forced them
back to the boat. There was no trace.

Slowly they began the tasks Brigha
gave them – the stones Uischa gathered
became low walls, clay was collected,
wood cut. Work was sluggish –
hearts were heavy, bodies beaten.
Brigha told them they must work
or die, none of them couldn't know
how long the summer months might last.

                        *

Then it was winter.
                  The speed with which
warmth and light left the land
terrified them. Only one
of the round-houses has a roof –
they huddled inside.

                The ice-storm came
without warning in the night –
relentless rain froze on all surfaces,
wrapped the world in a weight of ice –
birds fell dead from the sky,
birches, dragged down by it
bent to earth, black spruce sagged,
no creature stirred. The silence was worse
than the solid silence of the frozen sea,
broken by the boom of ice crags colliding.
They'd suffered so many terrible things,
come to a place they thought they knew,
but they didn't know it at all and now
the gods were going to make them pay.

When the brief sun finally broke through,
the crack of branches springing back

was the snapping jaws of shocking beasts
circling outside, watching and waiting.

*

Brigha was sick. Each day she got worse,
vomited the food the villagers fed her.
She hunched under skins and blankets –
too weak to tell them what to do,
she turned her face to the wall and wept.
Brendhan wet her lips with water,
dripped moisture into her mouth,
held her head as she spewed it back,
kept trying until she fell asleep.

Even though they eked out food
hunger haunted – children stopped crying,
the elders slept – each empty belly
clutched to try to stop the ache.

The outside world was iron hard,
sun barely rose before it sank back.

From the freezing silence outside the hut
soundless shapes crept towards them.
Sudden shouting, the loud clashing
of wood on wood, woke them. Brendhan
slipped from Brigha's side and went out.
The medicine man who cured the child
stood in the gloom, his people gathered
behind– their women kept children close,
men lowered weapons as Brendhan watched.

On the frozen earth in front of the hut
were several baskets and bowls of food –

dried fish, grain, a goose, fresh killed.
The man picked up a stick, snapped it
in four pieces, placed them by
the food. Then they left.

           Each fourth
day they came – sometimes carrying
a few eggs, game, a little more grain,
sometimes a salmon or strips of dried meat –
the hill-people came from their hut to thank them.
Brigha was dying, they knew that, but
they dare not use Uischa's words
to praise the strangers, show their gratitude,
instead the villagers vowed to honour
the debt they owed, in their own tongue.

That winter was longer, snow lay thicker
than ever the hill-folk had known back home.
The strangers in skins bought what food
they could spare. Children, first to fail,
grew stronger with the Bear People's gifts.
The Hegantii were hungry, some didn't survive,
but most made it through that terrible time.

Brigha's life lingered through those months –
neither alive nor dead, her eyes sunk deep
in her head. Brendhan stayed at her side,
giving her water and drops of bone broth,
cleaning her up when she gagged and spewed.

           *

The sickness slowed, then it stopped
but Brigha was in another world,
couldn't even care for herself –

shit scoured her skin. Brendhan
tried to keep her clean, warmed water
to wash her with. When he wiped
the raw red flesh she whimpered like
a wounded creature too weak to cry.

The women took over the washing from him,
gently smoothing on precious grease
to soothe her pain and heal the sores.
They rolled her over, saw her stomach,
saw the swelling, felt feet kick –
a baby would come within one full moon.
They placed Brigha's hand on her belly –
she was too far away to feel anything

> *where is she why has she gone she wouldn't leave me she*
> *wouldn't leave me she wouldn't leave me why has she gone*
> *she wouldn't leave me she wouldn't leave me shewouldn't*
> *leavemewouldn'tleavewouldn'tlllllll*

The baby began to make its way
into the ice world. Women hung blankets
round Brigha, told Brendhan they would do
what they could.
                      She couldn't stand
so they left her curled up on her side.
Hour after hour the women attended,
applied their ancient wisdom to aid
Brigha and the baby, pressed her belly
with each contraction, spoke the charms
and spells of the tribe, but no baby came.

When they saw that Brigha's body
was worn out, their faces, lit by firelight
were full of fear. They begged her to do

what the baby needed – she never responded.

Awne – born the year before
the twins – who had swum with them,
played on the cliffs, prayed with them,
who braided Brigha's long thick hair,
who taught them both the tribe's own words
for – *water   adder   mother* – Awne
took charge, told them they should turn her
onto her back. The older women
were shocked – she said they should do it now
and hold her up – they were too afraid.
Awne hauled Brigha over towards her –
her sister lifted Brigha's shoulders –
at the next spasm she pressed her hands
down on Brigha's belly – eyes opened
wide with pain and shock, Brigha screamed
her mother's name.   Feet appeared first –
two limp, purple legs slithered out –
hips – trunk – then everything stopped –
the baby was too big to be born.
Awne stared at the lifeless limbs –
her sister was shouting but the words
were a clatter of crow-squarks coming at her –
a muddle of noise that made no sense –
she looked up – a mouth was moving
in her sister's face, fast and angry,
but the sounds it made were mad crows –
I don't know what to do, she said –
Get it out! Get it out! the mouth yelled.
She shuddered – took the tiny body,
placed both hands around its hips –
Do it now! her sister screamed –
she turned it slowly to one side.

When they saw an arm, a shoulder,
the women gasped. Awne didn't wait
this time – turned the baby again –
the second shoulder came free – carefully
she slid her fingers inside, felt for
its face, eased it into the world,
sat stunned with the still child in her lap.
The older women took it from her
and the baby bawled, long and loud.

*

The tribe came, blinking, back to the world
with signs of spring. Awne wrapped
baby Dubn – they named her for the dark –
in her cloak and held her high
so she could see the sun rise slowly
out of the ocean, stretching East.

Neither Brigha's mind nor body
were whole – she didn't walk or speak
except to ask where Uischa was.
Her eyes were dull, she didn't know
her brother or the tribe, her breath
had the stale stink of sickness,
her lips were white, limbs flaccid,
her beautiful hair tangled and thin.
To the tribe she seemed to be suspended
somewhere between ice and sky –
the world of the living – the land of the dead.

When weather warmed Brendhan carried
Brigha to the ocean. To be
by the water was the only thing
that seemed to sooth his sister's torment.

He laid her down where waves lapped
at her feet – sometimes she stirred
as if she was far away and dreaming,
but Brendhan never knew for sure
whether she remembered water –
what the sea had been to both of them.

Awne and the women attended
to the baby and to Brigha.
When they brought her daughter to her,
held it to her breast she seemed
bewildered by it, couldn't hold it –
they saw its crying caused her hurt –
still, she allowed the child to suckle.

The hill-people knew now just how long
the summer months would warm this world.
They worked the land to plant their crops
of grain, they fished and gathered food.

Before they went to their summer grounds
the Bear People taught the tribe how they
hunted caribou, caught fat salmon.
In gratitude the hill-people gave them
an iron axe. They were amazed –
the copper they used made intricate items
but it wasn't as hard or as sharp as iron.

The Bear People called that place by the sea
Hahg-ha-whe so the Hegantii
took that name for their new home,
built strong round-houses to stand
the many frozen months of winter,
learned the lives of beasts and birds there,
learned which way the winds would blow,

when fish would spawn and when to pick
the sea urchins, the soft-shelled clams,
learned about wild berry bushes,
herbs to heal and flavour food.

*

When summer came Brendhan took Brigha
to the ocean. Often Awne
brought the child, who from the first
was entranced by water – who babble-talked
back to its intimate lap and lull,
shrieked with pleasure when it pounded
the shore, took her first tottering steps
from Awne's arms into the waves
and swam. For the first time Brigha
seemed to see the child, followed
its wriggling body as it bobbed
and paddled, rolled then righted, by
wave after wave. Brendhan watched –
when Dubn came close he carried Brigha
into the water near to the baby
then slowly let her go. She drifted
on her back, the baby beside her.

After that, when the weather was warm,
the sea gentle, they took them both
to the ocean. Every day Dubn
swam a little further and faster
away from her mother. The morning she dived
below the surface, Brigha slipped
from Brendhan's hold and followed the baby.
He let her go.   When the two of them
swam side by side out from the shore

and disappeared, Brendhan didn't
try to track them, to watch them together,
glimpse his dear sister – gone from him now –
as she had been – a stream of bright bubbles
circling, gliding, chasing and playing
under the water, back home in the waves.

On land it was different, Brigha languished –
didn't know anyone, didn't walk,
though the tribe tried time after time
to strengthen her legs, help her stand –
she didn't speak, but sometimes at night
they'd hear her muttering to Uischa
as if none of this had happened at all,
as if they were all on the island again,
back in the dunes with marram-grass blowing
and sand-violets growing and sea-holly flowers
burnishing air to a breath of blue.

Brendhan felt grief burrow like a louse
into his heart, hollow out a home there.

*

Year after year he carried Brigha
down to the tide to swim with her daughter
out of his sight with the dolphins and seals.

Some summer nights he'd stand in the water,
listen to harp seals bawling and barking –
sometimes he called to them so they'd come closer
but he never swam out in the wild sea again.

*

As Dubn grew she cared for Brigha,
helped to wash her, dress and feed her,
sat close by her chattering about
things she saw, her small, strong hands
wiping flecks from Brigha's face.
She'd prattle on about plants and animals –
the scuts of deer, the way birch trees
fuss in the wind, their flutter and hiss,
the broad flat beaks of snail-eating ducks,
what moss felt like under her feet,
how the Turtle Tribe made medicine from lichen
and taught her trees were *Standing People*,
told her the Turtle Tribe were once
sea creatures under an icy island
who left their home to walk the world
as men do on dry land. At times
she'd imitate the insects and birds –
a chirruping, buzzing cricket in summer,
a chittering woodchuck, the caribou's grunt
or call like geese flying over the forest.
And always attentive, asking questions.

She heard her people talk together
of the land they had to leave –
of Uischa who taught them the words
she bought with her – how she would sing
in the oak-grove to her own gods –
how they'd come to Hahg-ha-whe –
how the words had given hope
when they were lost in ice-bound oceans –
how Brigha saved them from the sickness
but banished her own mother, Uischa –
she repeated the things they said to Brigha
but Brigha didn't seem to hear.

Dubn didn't know why Brigha
forced Uischa from the tribe,
why she forbade them all from praying.
The Hegantii talked of evil spirits
who'd whispered bitter words to Brigha,
thoughts as sinuous as snakes,
and told her she must send her mother
far from the shores of Hahg-ha-whe
force her from the home they'd made there,
said Brigha's head and heart were weary,
she had no strength to fight them so
she'd done the thing the spirits said.

When Dubn asked Brendhan what had happened
he wouldn't answer – it was as if
the past was pointing, like an arrow
drawn and dangerous, in a bow
that might at any moment be loosed,
sever the threads that tied them together.
She felt her father's pain and fear
and never asked of Uischa again.

Instead, she told herself a story
of a ghost-child, Uischa, a girl
named for water, who wandered the woods
far from the sea which was her home.
Dubn would walk there, find Uischa,
play with her among the pine trees,
take her pebbles, sea-weed, shells,
talk to her of seals and salt,
of Brigha, Brendhan and the tribe.

One day she asked the ghost girl why
she couldn't come back to Hahg-ha-whe
the child touched her cheek and cried,

sang the words that Brendhan sang.

After that, although she searched
carrying her sea-gifts and calling,
Dubn didn't see Uischa again.

*

Through the time of her growing, Dubn
knew only that a terrible thing
had happened, saw her people's sadness,
went with Brendhan to the birch wood
when he urged Uischa's gods
to guide them, give them strength and knowledge,
prayed the gods would still protect them,
forgive them for the things they'd done.
She begged the tribe to follow Brendhan
one by one they went there with them,
stood together in the trees,
found some solace from their grief
as they said Uischa's sacred words.

Awne loved Dubn as a daughter –
when Dubn chose a man to marry
from the Bear Tribe, brought him home
to live with them, Awne sewed them
clothes of calf-skin – stitched three circles,
filled with wreaths of the marram and flowers
they'd left behind on their tiny island
and would never see again –
pink geraniums veined with purple,
sand-violet, sea-holly, burnet rose,
stitched the stars that traced their journey,
stitched the shapes of seals diving,
the tracks of beaver, caribou, bear,

the watchful eyes of fox and wolf,
stitched the strength of leaping salmon,
frost on grass and falling snow-flakes,
stitched the ocean, stitched the ice.

*

The children of the children's children
tried to hold their name, Hegantii,
and keep Uischa's sacred words safe.
They lived in peace with the Bear People
and the People of the Turtle,
lived their lives and left their bones
facing east – facing the sea.

*

Fog

Numeh was squatting in a shallow pool –
knees splayed, staring down
to see what still water might make
of the thing between her legs. She shifted
her weight, bent head and neck
forward, waited for water to settle.
Fleshy lumps came into focus –
mysterious ridges, mystifying folds,
puckered openings, pocks, dead-ends
that made it hard to work out what
was what. She poked into the parts
she couldn't see, found her pee hole,
wriggled her finger in. It hurt.

Water exploded in front of her face.
As she lost her balance, stumbled back,
loud laughter from the far bank
drowned out her squeal of surprise.
Fury filled Numeh, she floundered and splashed
towards the figure, fists flailing,
grabbed his hair and hit him hard.
Ma'khen laughed when she wrestled him
to the ground, pummelling and punching,
her teeth clenched, tears burning.

He held her arms behind her back,
You fight better than a boy,
but you blub and grizzle like a girl.
Suddenly she stopped. Ma'khen was wary,
You won't trick me, I know your traps,
if I let go, you'll leather me.
Numah's nose was running now,
she snorked and spat, but stayed still.
Ma'khen loosed his hold on her,
I only laughed because you looked
crazy trying to see your own cunt.
I didn't mean to make you cry,
I'm sorry I upset you, Numeh.
She turned to him, *You didn't*, she said.

They walked together through the wood,
neither spoke until they neared
Hahg-ha-whe. Numeh hacked
at nettles with a willow switch.
Whenever Ma'khen tried to talk
she swatted him hard with the stick.
I was going to say – Whack! –
the switch cut across his cheek,
the shock of it stopping him dead.
Numeh hurled her weight at him
then, quick and light as a lynx,
she flicked her foot behind his ankle,
flipped him over, flung him down,
straddled his chest and held his shoulders –
though he was bigger, bulkier than her
she was as strong as him. *I blub*
like a girl because I'm a girl –
the strongest girl that's ever been born
in all of the Agawhe people –
I'm stronger than any boy and that

includes you. But I am a girl!
She thrust her groin towards him,
held his face in both her hands –
Would you like to look for yourself?
And as she spoke, she had the urge
to tip him upside down as well –
to push her fingers into him,
see where everything went, what
was connected to what, what
someone else's secret flesh
felt like against her fingers.
No thanks Numeh, Ma'khen said.
I'm starving, let's go and find food.
Numeh laughed and let him go

        Ma'khen didn't mean to make things worse that day   we were friends
        to hear him laughing at me made me want to punch him hard
        Some of the kids would tease me   say my body was made wrong
        my fanny was too big   more like a willy   when I looked
        at some of the other girls' theirs were all different too
        mine was a bit more different that was all   I was as strong
        and fast as any boy and I could run and hunt with them
        if I chose to but I preferred to stay close to the camp
        working with the women and girls   we'd finish all the jobs
        then sit together talking   sewing   weaving   drinking tea
        those were the only times I felt the world was safe   I think
        I knew some dangerous thing was waiting up ahead for me
        every time I asked my mother – Was I like other girls
        she'd call me pretty daughter – braid my hair and say to me –
        Numeh you'll marry and have children of your own one day

        when I fought with Ma'khen got him on the ground and held
        his face   I couldn't see him
        I saw
        another ocean

I saw time spiraling away from me
earth gashing open under my feet
floods rising   people reaching out   children crying
*   I couldn't get to them*
I held my breath as they slipped under the surface
one by one
and somewhere in the horror   I thought   I thought

Then it all stopped and Ma'khen was whingeing on about
how hungry he was   I was glad   I thought maybe I'd been
asleep and dreaming to see such shocking things   I didn't tell him
what I thought I'd seen

*   When I got home Grandmother said –*
Numeh   it has begun
I didn't know what she meant
all she'd tell me was that she had known from the moment
of my birth the ancestors had chosen me   that I
was going to be the keeper of our history the servant
of our gods   I said I wouldn't do it
told her she was wrong
she stroked my hair   said it wasn't up to me
the spirits knew the ancestors' blood ran deep in me
that I must keep their promise   hold the words safe for the tribe

Numeh was not a child to show
disrespect or disobey
the elders. In the light of each
full moon they went together to
the great tree that grandmother chose
because she said the ancestors
held that place in high regard.
Wrapped by night Numeh would
listen to Grandmother Umma, let
the strange words make their shapes around her.

Although Umma never asked her
to repeat them or told Numeh
what the meaning of them was,
Numeh could taste them, smell them, see them
circling, drifting in the dark.

In her nineth summer Numeh let
the hasp of her child's heart slide open
and the ancient sounds slip in.

*

As Numeh grew, Grandmother's strength
began to fail, but her spirit stayed strong.
When she was too weak to walk
Numeh knelt close, held her hand
as Umma uttered the sacred words.
Numeh swore she'd try to keep
the words safe, hold them for the tribe.

The year had turned, birch trees yellowed
and autumn fog crept from the ocean
when Umma went to the Spirit World.

Another winter was approaching,
there was much work they must do.

Some of the tribe were strangely troubled,
felt silent danger creeping closer
from the east. The elders said
there was nothing new to harm them,
only winter's ice-packed ocean,
they must make ready for the freeze
and pray and offer up those things
the gods demanded.

       As days diminished
some could not shake off their dread,
lay wide awake in winter houses
as others slept. A few men sharpened
weapons as the women held
children closer to their chest.
Sleep for them was shadows flitting –
their black-ringed eyes could barely rest.

Through the lengthening night they heard
song of ice-berg, song of blizzard,
heard the scratch of scuttling squirrels,
heard rabbits shriek when weasels pounced,
heard gekkering fox, the howl of wolf
and nothing else.
                 The elders said
mistrust would make the spirits angry,
they'd be punished. Numeh said nothing
but she heard on Hahg-ha-whe
something that was like a sound,
something like the sea remembering.
She thought of Grandmother, those words –
and once again the world ripped open,
earth and sky and sea changed places,
the ground below was giving way
as suffocating fog rolled round her.
When she tried to scream for Ma'khen
to grab her, hold her, stop her falling
she felt Umma's old words stirring –
rising up in her throat until
they flew from her – she couldn't stop them –
guttural, stuttering, senseless sounds.

Those who were awake and waiting
lit the lamps and gathered round her–

shocked and scared, the sleepers woke.

People started to creep closer –
a young man lunged at Numeh yelling
they should kill her, she was possessed
by evil spirits because she wasn't
normal – he clutched at her clothes,
tried to drag her to the door.
They seized him, said Numeh was
a child of the tribe, the voice
was Numeh's voice, not vengeful demons,
the tribe must listen, let her speak.

As the quartz-white quarter moon rose
the noise that came from Numeh changed–
fragments formed that might have meaning,
sounds they thought they knew were shaping,
like the language of their people.

The waxing moon had long since set
when Numeh stood, started to speak –

Before our tribe learned language, they lived with the animals of the world in a place far away. Sometimes people had human shape, sometimes they took the shape of seal or caribou, or lynx or crow and though they were as swift and strong as any creature, they were not content because they had no human words, just the sounds of the creatures they copied. The spirits lived in all things and the Great Spirit, who was wiser, older than any, saw all things.

There lived in that world a wild Wind who spent his time chasing clouds and howling above high mountain peaks. One day he grew tired – he sat down on the top of the tallest mountain, looked out at the land for the first time and saw the shining Water below him. She was so beautiful and so still that Wind fell in love. He flew to Water, asked her to be his wife but she was afraid of Wind, he disturbed her – she loved all the people and animals that lived in the world, she would not be the wife of the Wind for their sake – if they laid together, he'd let loose his fierce power, floods would follow and everything would die. Wind promised not to harm them so she let him kiss her tenderly, touch her skin with fingers soft as blossom, stroke her until she forgot the world, forgot what would happen if she listened too long, so lost she was in her love for the Wind. He breathed over her, she became cloud, flew with him, higher and higher they circled, cloud wrapped Wind, Wind grasped cloud in his great arms until the Wind cried and the cloud cried, felt herself turning to Water again, falling and flooding the whole world.

Wind begged his wife not to look but she turned around, saw land awash, people and animals swamped and drowning, waves crashing, whales stranded, fish floundering on mountain tops, birds, dead from hunger, falling out of the sky. She wept for them. When Wind was quiet once more Water became many streams and began to search for any creature still alive. She found a few animals and people, found the great gray seal – they cried bitterly for the flooded world but she was wife of Wind for all time.

When a child was born, they called her Oisca – child of Wind and Water. The Great Spirit loved the girl and gave her the secret language of the spirits, sent her to teach the people to talk, told her to teach her children's children, told her to hold the words in her heart.

Oisca kept the sacred words safe, taught them to the people who could now give themselves a name. They chose –Hegantii – People of the Hill. She taught them to her son and daughter who were Brendan and Briga, who loved the sea more than the land.

Terrible torrents of rain fell – the land was like a poisoned lake – everyone was starving and sick. No-one could live in that place but they were too frightened to leave. They begged Oisca to stop the sick-

ness with her songs and prayers so they could live for all time in their land.

Oisca's prayers did not have power to prevent such pestilence. The Great Spirit was filled with sadness to see so many dead and dying so he gave a gift to Briga – gave the of skill of swift and swallow to wing their way across wide oceans – made her restless as an albatross so she would steer them over the sea, take them to another world.

When the words stopped Numeh sank down,
slept until the moon had risen.

As she slept a huge storm swept in,
waves like mountains smashed the shore-line,
so powerful was the wind that people
thought it was about to tear them
from earth and hurl them at the heavens.
Some were sure that Numeh's soul
had been stolen – her father begged
the shamans to kill her body but keep
her name so that her soul could come back
to the tribe and live again.

The world outside was crash and chaos,
while in the hut, it was as if
time itself was tangled tightly
with their fear and had forgotten
how to flow. Like frozen fog,
sound and movement were suspended,
spores of terror spread amongst them –
with each breath, they breathed them in.

First to move was Numeh's mother,
leaned across to touch her daughter,
Numeh stirred – the spell of silence

splintered as the air around lurched
sideways with the weight of voices –
children crying, people pleading
with the shamans to shield them from
the evil spirits now in Numeh
that had called down storms to kill them.
The words of those who would protect her
were drowned out by their desperation.

Moon-light lit the hut when Ma'khen
opened the door – the world outside
stood still, the sky was clear of cloud,
new snow blued the glittering ground.
He too was shaken by what had happened,
didn't know what he should do –
his friend Numeh was now becoming
one of the spirit people – the tribe
were waiting for someone or something
to break the spell and ease their shock.
Ma'khen's mouth tried to make words
but no words came. His brother Karrik
stood beside him, whispered to him,
We're all scared brother, but Numeh has
a different way of knowing the world –
she's one of us but also one of
the spirit people. Numeh is suffering,
this might be too much for one person,
she didn't ask for any of it.
You are a good friend, Numeh knows that,
knows she can trust you. And we need to
understand what's happening to us,
where Numeh words and that strange story
came from. Ma'khen you are young
but you must help her – you have to speak.

Karrik's kind words helped his brother
find courage to face the fearful tribe –
Numeh never brought the storm winds,
Ma'khen told them, *the words she spoke*
she learned from Umma, who was wise –
she taught the sacred words to Numeh
because our tribe has lived so long
with the People of the Turtle
and the Bear Folk and forgotten
who our own ancestors are –
because she knew they would be safe
in Numeh's heart until we need them.
If Numeh speaks them it's because
we will need to know ourselves –
who we are and where we came from.

He turned towards the listening shamans –
You alone can ask the spirits
to tell the tribe what we should do.
Please, go to your secret places,
carry out your ceremonies,
seek the spirits' wishes, ask them
if Numeh's words are wise and true.

In the hut Numeh was waking –
dried spit crusted at the corners
of her mouth, her hair a mass
of knots and tangles stuck with sweat
to her scalp. She staggered upright –
when she tried to speak her voice
was the creak of wind-blown branches.
Her mother held water to her lips
but Numeh didn't seem to know
what to do and wouldn't drink.
Unsteady and dazed, she stared out at

the frightened faces – her mother moistened
her dry lips – Numeh drank, not taking
her eyes from them. When she could speak
she asked her father why they were
all watching her. He shrank away.
She asked her mother what had happened,
who tore her clothes? No answer came.
Instead her mother wrapped her warmly,
held her until she slept once more.

The shaman returned – said the spirits
had watched and listened when Umma sat
under the great tree, taught her grandchild
the language the Great Spirit gave them
when the world was new – the story
Numeh had told them was their history,
her words held the tribe's long-ago truth.

In lamp and fire light, in uneasy
quiet, the name *Hegantii* hovered-
touched the tribe's deep buried dreams,
washed like waves the shores of memory,
brought the strange smell of a metal
they'd thought was nothing more than myth.

Breath began to slow and steady –
the tribe talked softly to one another
of their old name, of other seas,
of dark water in dunes pools and
a blue shimmer of summer light.

*

After that Numeh never
left the shore. She stared into

the half-light not speaking or sleeping.
Ma'khen bought her food and fed her,
helped her mother change wet clothes
for dry, though Numeh didn't seem
to feel the chilling grip of fog,
the ravage of hunger, the rasp of thirst.

Gradually, as day-light lengthened,
people came cautiously to the beach,
curious to see the silent girl
who sat and watched the waves. Most were
too afraid to look at her face –
some said her family should send her
far away from Hahg-ha-whe,
she would arouse the spirits' anger –
others waited and listened with her,
though they saw only seal and sea-bird,
heard wash of waves, the sigh of wind.

All that spring she watched and waited,
fear gripping in her guts
like a fist – what she heard was
the breathing of some new beast coming,
slithering over sea towards them,
its skin was pocked with watching eyes,
stitched with lips stretched thin over
its grin of teeth. Numeh never
answered when they asked her what
was out there on the endless ocean,
asked if Sedde, goddess of sea,
was angry, planned to punish them
by sending sea-beasts to their shore.

As summer approached most of the tribe
had lost interest – no loathsome thing

had crawled from the sea to snatch their children,
the spirits hadn't caused crops to die,
sickness hadn't stalked among them.

Winter was nearing and families were
all returning from their autumn hunt.
Women were just beginning their work
the morning Numeh made her way
to the meeting place in the middle of
the village. They hadn't heard her voice
for so long they were shocked when she spoke –
Change is coming to Hahg-ha-whe,
a violent thing is creeping closer,
you must get ready and go at once.

Tumult swept through the whole village –
people quarrelling, shouting questions –
some were furious, others frightened –
Numeh walked back to the beach.
They followed like a flock of geese
flapping and honking after her,
jostling, asking, demanding answers.

As the sun climbed higher their clamour
diminished as dread took hold – first thoughts,
then voices became brittle – each word
was the sharp crack of bone snapping.

They could see nothing but now they knew
Numeh was right. The shamans' rituals
weren't enough for whatever was
coming towards them. Yet, they couldn't leave.
They implored Numeh to ask the ancestors
for protection – to pray to Oisca
to shield and shelter them from harm,

keep their home on Hahg-ha-whe
safe. She looked at them and said,
*This place does not belong to our tribe –
no-one owns the land – the land
owns us* – then turned to the horizon,
broken by the bows of boats
that came towards them with watching eyes –
the beast they dreaded, drawing nearer
with jutting teeth and jaws agape.
When they saw it, they turned their backs –
fled the shore-line, fled the land
where they'd hunted, fished and foraged,
where the bones of all the ancestors
had laid for a thousand autumns –
walked west towards a different water,
west to where the land was patterned
by the buffalo's beaten paths.

*

> *when we started out on our long walk I had no women's bleed*
> *I didn't like my body being different   I was*
> *a girl no matter what some of the other children said*
> *when an Agawhe girl begins their bleeding the shamans*
> *put on their ceremonial dress   perform their rituals*
> *drum and dance   everyone's happy   women dress the girl's hair*
> *in the adult manner   give her tokens   little carvings*
> *special shells   a button carved from bone   then she's presented*
> *with the grown-up clothes her mother has been sewing for her*
> *since her seventh year and her new body is celebrated*
> *for five days*

> *I could feel my body changing   I wanted it to change   I wanted it*
> *to stay the way it was   what if it*
> *turned into a man's and I had to live in it like that*

I thought if I ignored it   covered it up
then I could stop things happening to it
I always kept it hidden from the tribe
wouldn't even let my mother see me without my clothes

and all the time they wanted me to ask Oisca's help
the shamans carved a mask for me   I learned their rituals
they said I held the ancient sacred knowledge of our people
I told them they were wrong I didn't remember anything
my only gift was that I was more animal than most
that somehow I could smell a new and threatening thing before
it got too close
all I wanted
was to sit with the women   sewing   chatting   drinking tea
Umma's words were sounds I didn't understand

I didn't want to be different   I wanted to belong

I knew I never would

*

Fleeing Hahg-ha-whe for
their lives when winter was closing in
was frightening. They grabbed what food
and clothing they could carry, gathered
a few tools and treasured things,
harnessed dogs and hurried children
onto sleds. The boats they travelled
in when ice unfroze were useless
in the winter but they took two
so they could row the lake and rivers
they knew they'd need to cross next spring.
Snow lay thin, the boats and sleds
snagged on tussocks of grass and shrubs

time after time. Panic drove them
to drag and haul weight heavier than any
they'd managed to move before. Each thing
that couldn't be carried at speed was thrown
as they tried to lighten the loads.

They needed snow but no snow fell,
instead the wind thrashed them, whipped
skin raw, forced backs to bend
as they fought to keep on pressing forward.
It lifted up the lightweight boats
and flung them like dry autumn leaves.
One birch frame was badly broken –
they had to strip what precious skins
they could salvage from its structure
to help repair the remaining boat.

They were too scared to stop – when anyone
fell and couldn't get up again
someone else climbed from the sled
or lifted out a child to carry
and made room for them. Every moment
they believed whatever the strange boats brought
must ride on monstrous beasts towards them
or swoop down from the sky to snatch them.
Only when the sled dogs were done in
they found what cover they could and tried
to rest. But dread drove sleep away
even from their exhausted bodies.
They urged Numeh to ask for Oisca's
help, speak to the shamans, beg
the spirits to protect the tribe

> *I couldn't pray*
> *I didn't know the words   didn't understand*

any of the things Umma had said

that first winter of our flight I dreamed again
the sky fell
earth opened its great maw
and swallowed it   I was
no longer made of solid flesh   I felt my bones dissolve
and I became a cold formless drifting thing   lifted from sea
like fog
in every dream I heard   the distant barking of a seal

At first they knew the land – had hunted
there each summer since before times –
knew that the groups whose hunting grounds
they crossed would winter on the coast.

Then they were in strange surroundings –
higher ground, grim and gloomy,
that seemed to spread to the horizons –
a sodden plain that reeked of rot
and shuddered when they stepped on it.
Their pursuers would pick them off with ease
but they found no route around it,
feared their chasers closing in –
there was no choice, they had to cross.

They scoured the ground, gathered up
what branches and bushes they could find –
there were nowhere near enough.
For days the tribe spread out and searched
for any materials that might make
a track so they could cross the bog.
Trees were felled, shrubs torn up,
reeds and course grass were collected,
taken to the marsh, where women

and children soaked them, stripped them, made them
supple enough to twist and tie,
to weave and fasten, knot, then fashion
mats so they could cross the marsh.

Tentatively, young men trod
on the quivering track, moved on
until they found a firmer patch
with sufficient space to hold
a few people and their possessions,
somewhere that seemed a little less like
it would gulp them down in one go

> *when they went into the bog I felt a sudden sickness   what if*
> *someone took a step too far and sank so quickly*
> *that no-one had time pull them out*
> *in that place water and earth*
> *were the same dangerous thing – a mud hag – dragging people down*
> *I imagined it gripping feet   calves   thighs*
> *filling noses and mouths*
> *squeezing breath from soft bodies*
>
> *I caught a glimpse of Ma'khen as they worked*
> *even in that poor light I knew him by the way he moved*
> *him and Karrik together all day slogging side by side*
> *I felt my own strength bristle   my skin stretch with trying*
> *to hold it in   saw my hands put down the weaving*
> *I walked the narrow line of mats into the bog   some of the men*
> *shouted that I should leave   my doing men's work*
> *would only make the spirits angry*
> *I ignored them   made my way to Ma'khen and Karrik*
> *started work   no-one stopped me and together we edged forward*
> *testing   dragging ourselves on bellies across*
> *the quaking ground*

Some sobbing, others praying
the tribe stepped on the shaking bog.
It took three days to heave themselves,
their sleds and dogs to solid ground.

The world the tribe saw stretching out
in front of them was so immense
it made them dizzy for a moment –
rows of wooded hills reached west,
their bases vanishing into valleys
where long slashes of deep shadow
hid whatever was waiting for them.
And on a wide, green plain – water –
spilling down slopes, rushing in rivers,
lying in strings of streams and lakes.
On the horizon high peaks shone white.

The plateau dropped down steeply to
the tree-line. In between, a tide
of rock and rubble that skittered away
when they tried to walk on it.
The journey down was dangerous
but finally, they felt their feet
steadied by lichen and tiny tufts
of grasses growing in the gravel.
The smell of spruce after the stench
of the morass was wonderful.

That night was the first time they
set up camp since they'd escaped –
the first time they could talk together
of their future. A few wanted
to return to Hahg-ha-whe,
fight the brute the sea brought to them.
The shamans went together to some

secret spot among the trees –
Numeh hung back in the hope
that they'd forget her – what she wanted
was to sit with the girls and women,
talking together, plaiting hair –
they did not forget and Numeh
took her mask and went with them.

When what sun there was had risen,
they came back to camp and told them
the spirits saw a dreadful danger
if they went home to Hahg-ha-whe,
said Oisca spoke again through Numeh,
said they were Hegantii, they had
left their land and crossed an ocean,
they must travel on once more.

Numeh was too numb with tiredness
to answer all their many questions –
too exhausted even to cry,
she lay down where she was and slept.

*

They were vigilant, wary, watchful,
night and day they took turns to guard.
Tribes who spent the summer there
would be gone but bands of hunters
might still be stalking, making the most
of what light was left. They were always aware
that whatever was chasing might close in
on them if they dropped their guard.
Among the trees they felt less frightened,
the going was easier where the ground
that had been soft mounds of spruce needles

became beds of birch and rowan leaves.

As they came from the forest they saw
a massive river flowing fast
round jagged rocks that spiked the surface,
turned the shallows to violent vortices
they couldn't cross with the sleds.

They'd have to hold off for winter ice
so they made camp, set up their tents
where whatever hunted them, beast
or man, might miss the signs that they
were there. All of them listened like owls,
hesitated like hares. Now and then noises –
a click that could be caribou hooves –
barks that might be fox – or follower –
stopped the breath in every body.
Children were told to stay in tree cover,
men set hidden traps for fish,
women went on restoring the ripped hull
of their only boat, stitched the skins
they'd saved and made the vessel sound.

It was full moon before the river froze.
They waited seven more days then made
their winding way round spears of rock.
Numeh worked hard next to Ma'khen
and Karrik as they carried children,
heaved sleds that held the sick and old,
pulled and lugged. When she struggled
Ma'khen tried to help, each time
she shoved him away. They slogged on
until the whole tribe had hauled itself
up the bank on the opposite side,
set up a spot to eat and rest.

Ma'khen put his hand on Numeh's
arm, pulled her quietly away
from camp. Sky had started turning
its night-wheel – stars scribed their way
as they stood together watching them.
What is it you're so scared of Numeh?
he asked. *Nothing,* Numeh snapped,
I'm not afraid of anything.
You're scared of something, Ma'khen said.
Numeh was silent for a while.
I'm scared of what they think I am –
some kind of shaman- a 'wise woman'
they call me – that's a laugh –
I'm scared because they say I talk
to the ancestors – I never knew
what Umma was saying, it was all
just noise to me, none of it
made any sort of sense – I'm scared
they've convinced themselves I can
show them the future, read the past,
tell them what they need to know –
I can't do any of that, I'm just...
He ran his finger along her lips,
she jerked her head away from him.

They squatted down together in silence.
You prayed Numeh, talked of things
we had forgotten – said we call
ourselves 'Agawhe,' the tribe who live
on Hahg-ha-whe, but we're 'Hegantii'
and we crossed oceans, crossed the world.
At first you spoke a language filled with
words we couldn't understand,

*it scared the shit out of everyone but
the longer we listened the more sense you made.
Again and again you've left this world,
gone with the spirits and gods somewhere,
brought the ancestors back to us,
brought the name 'Hegantii' to us –
now they trust you, that's why they call you
'wise woman' – you're wise Numeh.
But am I a woman?* Numeh asked.
Ma'khen touched her lip, looked at her.
She wiped her mouth with the back of a hand,
spat out on snow and strode away.

At first light the lookouts saw
strangers, sounded the alarm.
Almost at once the whole tribe
were ready to repulse an attack
though they were obviously outnumbered.

The elders instructed everyone
to leave their weapons lowered and wait –
the strangers may not mean them harm.
Their Shamans, carrying charms, stepped forward,
the elders walked unarmed until
they stood a few feet from the man
who must be chief, and welcomed him.
He replied – they didn't recognize
most of the words but knew that they
were being welcomed in return.

Formalities of friendship made,
weapons were warily laid aside.
The new-comers' chief was talking,
pointing certain people out –
they knew he was asking about them

but couldn't work what he wanted
to know, the language too unlike
their own. The shamans sought out Numeh,
took her to the chief and told her
to translate what was said – she stared
in disbelief – *I can't, I don't know
their tongue, it's meaningless to me,*
she stuttered and tried to leave. The shamans
said the gods had given her
the power to unravel and understand
other languages not their own –
she must hold her hearing open,
listen and let the words find ways
to make their meaning clear to them.

The chief began again – this time
he turned to Numeh, spoke more slowly.
And slowly, sound by sound, the words
unwound themselves so she could hear them
in her own tongue. Hesitant
and stumbling, she began to speak –
*The visitor says the next valley
leads to a pass, a path through mountains,
across plains to where their people
have hunted since the world was new.
He says the stories of their tribe
tell of pale-skinned people from
a different world – like them, but not
like them – some had dark hair while some
were lighter, more like winter grass,
and a few among them had hair
the colour of polished copper – 'fox-red'
he calls it. They have come to see
if we are those pale-skinned people.*

One thousand years on Hahg-he-whe,
the Hegantii had learned to live
in rain and fog, in winter freeze,
swum in summer seas with seals,
married with Bear and Turtle tribes,
lost their stories, lost their name,
lost their ancestors, become Agawhe.
Still, sometimes, the ancients looked
from their eyes – a face becoming
a mirror holding its own history –
Numeh's hair was from Bear forefathers
but her skin was fairer, her eyes flecked
with shades of blue and streaks of gray.

He stared at Numeh, said a few words –
no-one moved and no-one spoke –
no-one dared look at another –
perhaps these people had come to kill them
because they carried different blood?

Numeh pulled her hood back from
her head, pushed up her sleeve, held out
the inside of her arm to him.
She trembled at the thought that he
could seize her, hold her captive – kill her.
His gaze moved from wrist to eyes,
he slid a hand into his clothing,
held out a figure, finely sculpted.
She took it from him, gave a gasp –
still no-one moved.
                        Numeh stared
down at her palm – a female figure,
her tiny body bone pale,
her hair sculpted, finely scored
and stained as rust-red as a fox.

She had no legs, instead she had
the lower body and back flippers of
a seal. Numeh folded her fingers
round it, held it to her heart.

Then she heard the chief speak to her.
He wants to know what we are called.
The elders and shamans talked together –
Tell them we're Hegantii people,
who left our land and sailed the sea,
who've lived so long on Hahg-he-whe,
we've come to call ourselves Agawhe.
Say we've lived in peace and listened
to the Great Spirit, given offerings,
honoured all animals of earth and water,
all rocks and trees – we're travelers now
who love and respect the land like them.
She answered as the elders asked.

In the long silence that followed Numeh
saw the world as if she was looking
through a sheet of solid ice –
every shape etched sharp as if
carved from the air – the chief, his clothes,
her hand, her tribe, each broken blade
of grass, each single flake of snow,
every speck of white that circled
the raven's eye – she saw rocks
dissolve – heard hibernating woodlice
breathing in leaf litter, so clearly
that her heart flooded, filled with love
for their little curled-up lives.

It might have been a month, a moment
or a day before he answered –

at the sound the world snapped back
and Numeh listened attentively,
translated what was said –
They are
'Re'wa'ki' Red- Earth People,
from the western lakes and forests.
Like us they had to leave – fierce tribes
arrived – attacked them – terrible things –
bodies dishonored, relics desecrated –
their homes, their hunting grounds, were stolen,
they have travelled far since then.
They've got nothing of their past
except their stories – and this small thing –
she showed them the object, turned it over
in her palm. They stared – *Who is she?*
Numeh offered the beautiful object
back to the chief, told him the elders
asked who she was.
A water spirit –
her name is Fri'he – Fish-Woman –
without her we wouldn't survive.
She came to us from before-time stories –
when the giants had gone, the stories say,
there was no food, we were starving –
she came – half human, half strange fish –
helped us find food in lakes and rivers –
she saved us then, she saves us now.
We took her with us when we ran.

She looked around at the strangers –
their weariness, the weight of their loss –
felt for a moment the sudden surge
of tenderness she'd felt for the woodlice.
Then terrible anger – rage raced through her –
every nerve of Numeh's body

wanted to fight them, force away
the pitiful tale the chief had told –
their watching, their questions, their sorrow, their seal-woman,
their need to know, the threat they brought –
such fury! The chief saw her face change –
he stepped back – his tribe tensed,
eyes went to weapons. Ma'khen spoke –
You're safe now Numeh, we're all safe,
you've done what the spirits wanted,
we're safe.
My skin though Ma'khen...
I showed him my skin...what if he...
if they...I shouldn't have shown him my skin...
Her eyes were wide with fear. Ma'khen
stood closer to her, held her shoulders –
You've been to the world where we can't follow
but you're back now and we're all safe.
Sit down and rest.
She couldn't rest –
anger became agitation.
He helped her sit but she couldn't stop
plucking at the sleeve of her parka,
as if insects were infesting it,
pulling at it, at them – trying
to cover up – un-show herself.

Ma'khen gestured to the man
that they should all sit down too.

Once he felt danger diminish
Ma'khen pushed back his parka hood
and every one of the Red-Earth tribe
drew breath so sharply it was one sound.
He let them look, took his knife,
handed it, handle first,

to the chief, separated a strand
of his own hair and held it out
in invitation. The man hesitated –
Ma'khen nodded and the man
took hold of the hank of hair,
sliced it off and held it high –
lit by sun, it hung there shining –
the rich red-brown of a fox

> *I only remember exhaustion   and that carving*
> *the seal-woman*
> *when I held it   it didn't feel like a solid thing*
> *it was more like I was holding an idea   maybe*
> *a memory*
>
> *he called her Fish-Woman but I could see*
> *she was a seal*
> *when I asked where she came from he said The Dream Stories*
> *I tried to explain she was a creature of the air like us*
> *I'm not sure he understood*
>
> *they stayed seven days   we talked of journeys and of home*
> *I said I didn't believe we owned the land our people*
> *lived on   it was only lent to us by the spirits*
> *and if the spirits sent us from it we had to go*
> *to start out on a new journey he shook his head   asked me*
> *why I said such things   said they believed that if they laid*
> *the bones of their ancestors down   entrusted them to that*
> *piece of ground   the spirits would let them stay for all time*
>
> *he had questions   who told me these things about the land*
> *how did I know the language of his tribe*
> *I couldn't answer*
> *I didn't know*
> *he asked who our First People were*

where were their bones
I asked the elders what I was to say
they said I must tell the story I'd told the tribe
the night of the great storm when the spirits first came to me

I didn't remember
so they told it again and I repeated it
word for word
I knew nothing of all that but when they talked about the seal
I found myself thinking once again about the carving
she was there and very real but not there   and not real
I could feel huge sadness in her   she was heavy with it
I wanted to comfort her   thinking of it made me cry

I had to tell them how we found our language and our name
that I was keeper of the sacred words
I felt so sick when I said that   if I could
I'd have run away right then   I hated the way everyone expected me
to know important things   Ma'khen said I must have learned
wisdom from Umma   that she had made a path for me
to the world of spirits but I knew for sure
I'd never been there   if I had I know I would have seen
Umma again and there's no way I'd have forgotten that

*

Many times, the threat they'd fled from
seemed less terrifying than
anything lying ahead might be.
Months passed, every ear and eye
strained for the slightest sign of danger.
They talked together less and less
as they glimpsed the truth that they would never
go back home to Hahg-ha-wh –
the space that shore had taken up

in them was echo and emptiness –
something silent was creeping in –
a loss – a liquid sort of sorrow
was there – weak as winter shadows –
but there. And if anyone
had words to name it, no-one did.

The Red- Earth people had told of tribes
who would harm them, places where
they could be killed by collapsing cliffs,
where giant earth bulls crowded below ground,
which rivers ran too wild for crossing,
where food was scarce or water foul –
told too of great lakes full of fish,
plains alive with wandering animals,
of honey hidden in hollow logs,
of land good for growing grain.
They warned the tribe again and again
not to go North of the Red Mountains,
the place they left, their Red Earth land.
Though it was good and generous
it had become blood lake, bone scatter –
The Place of Tears, they called it now.
The elders wanted to know why they
didn't choose some suitable place
they'd found in their flight and settle there.
They followed where Fish-Woman took them,
they said, she wanted them to find
the pale-skinned people, now they could search
for somewhere the spirits would welcome them
let them settle, let them rest.

Before they left, the Red Earth leader
gave Numeh a gift – a figure – their Fish-Woman,
carefully copied and carved from wood.

She treasured her through all their travels –
sometimes, where she was alone,
she talked to her of sea and seals,
sang the songs the women sang.

*

They felt their way forward – they were
sentinel, scout, seeker of omens,
watcher, reader of cloud and raindrop,
bird flight and paw-print. Sleep was a stranger,
speech shriveled, they were fretful
as ghosts, moved like ghosts,
disturbed nothing, left no trace.

Through that winter Numeh thought
about her body, Ma'khen's body,
other bodies – what those bodies
might feel like to touch, to move
against – their smell, their bulk,
the weight of them, their bend and flex,
their possibilities – what they
might look like lying side by side.

What they might look like?
                          What did she
look like? Her breasts had grown like girls
her age, but she had short, fine hair
like fluff on her body, while her face
was darkened with down on chin and lip,
she could feel it sprouting, it's
determined growth disgusted her.
She scraped at it with a sharp blade
until her jaws were sore and scabbed.
The bulge in her fanny, the throat-apple

she felt in her neck sickened her.

When her woman's bleed began
she sobbed, thanked Seal-Woman,
thanked the spirits, told no-one.

Coiled up inside those thoughts,
that dread of being different,
other ideas were incubating –
the muscle-tightening, limb-lengthening,
bone-hardening in her body
made her hot, made her restless,
made her fingers seek out soft flesh
to probe its possibilities.

For Numeh nothing had ever felt real,
nothing certain, nothing clear,
but what happened when she touched
and stroked, started to make sense –
her body, her weird, ugly body,
was a dropped pot she was putting
back together bit by bit –
her legs when she ran, skimming the earth,
felt stronger, less shameful –
the power in her spine, her shoulders,
was slowly becoming a wonderful thing.

Now she was starting to trust herself –
she let the spirits talk to her,
went with the shamans when they asked her.
If ominous omens troubled the tribe,
and elders asked for her advice
she stopped denying she could help,
let her mind and spirit loose.

*

When the attack came, they were ready.
Numeh knew menace was moving closer,
warned them they should stay watchful –
for many days she'd felt it following –
prowling, stalking, slipping away,
before the scouts had seen a sign.

The small band that sprang from the dawn
were pitiful – bodies emaciated, eyes
hollow with hunger. They fought with ferocity –
the courage of those with no other chance,
the daring of the desperate.
The elders told Numeh not to fight –
they needed her, she must stay safe,
she took no notice of what they said.

The sun was hardly above the high peaks
when the fighting was all finished.
Six men went to the spirit world –
one from the Hegantii tribe,
five strangers lay – thin limbs twisted,
they sprawled over outcrops of stone,
shaved heads lolling horribly
in the early light. One looked
too old to fight, another was only
nine or ten – a child.

                    Numeh leaned
on the bent trunk of a white birch
way beyond the low ridge where
the ambush had happened. She clutched the tree,
breath rapid, heart racing,
beating so hard she thought any attackers

still living would be sure to hear it.

There must be more? It was madness
to risk a raid with so few fighters.
She had to hang on, there must be more?
Her knees were not able to hold her up,
she slid to the ground as the world slipped away.

*

A strange bird was shrieking inside
her skull – a single note – an alarm –
flooding ears, toes, the tips of fingers.

chr noto cc   ca ca ca
chr noto cc   ca ca ca

Her leg was so cold – as if someone
had taken her boot, pulled back her clothes.
But hot too   burning   burning like –

her heel was held in someone's lap,
someone squeezed the side of her thigh –
the burning flared – the bird shrieked –

chr noto cc   ca ca ca

the same notes searing her thigh –

chr noto cc   ca ca ca
chr noto cc   ca ca ca

The bird was trying to talk but it's voice
was buzzy and its beak drilled deep
into her thigh – when she tried

to shake it off its claws clung firm.

Try not to kick if you can –

                        Ma'khen
bent towards the burning place –
she shuddered, tried to cover herself –
he flicked her feeble hand away –
Stop kicking and keep still Numeh,
you're making it bleed more by wriggling.
He sat back briefly on his heels,
I don't think there's anything else in it.

Numeh tried to lift her leg –
the bird screamed – her head spun –
Ma'khen, get me something to stop it!
He set her foot on the soil – she groaned.
When you stop making it bleed, he said.
Anger tore through, she tried to hit him –
I swear I'll kill you – get me something!
Ma'khen blew out a long breath –
You know what? You're hard work Numeh.
He stood behind her shoulders,
Right, get up, we've got to get back.
She glared – *How am I supposed to get up?*
I'm far too heavy for you to lift.
He slipped his forearms under her armpits
and got her upright in one go –
Don't talk stupid, he said and tucked
his shoulder so she could lean on him –
Get moving girl. She did as he said.

They were a fair distance from the tribe,
pain and weariness made progress slow.
What were you doing out here? he asked.

There had to be more, she snapped, *I was searching.*
He sighed, *you had a spear in your leg,*
I saw it happen, how did you get
right out here?
                I ran, she said.
He shook his head in disbelief,
You went off on your own with a spear wound
to find more people to fight on your own.
Numeh reached round, nipped the flesh
of his armpit as hard as she could,
There might have been hundreds, she said.
Five, Ma'khen said. *They hadn't a hope.*
Plus women and kids – poor things were hiding
in a spinney, starving and scared.
How many – where are they? she wanted to know.
They're with the elders, two women, three kids.
Two girls, I'd guess about six or seven,
and a new-born baby boy.
The smallest girl tried to bite the shaman
when he gave her food – made me think of you.

Are you saying you hung around
watching kids when I was still missing?
she demanded. He shrugged his shoulders –
she tried to hit him.
                Those who weren't wounded
took turns to stand guard or to look for you –
you were missing for ages.
                How long? she asked.
More than two days – I didn't think
you'd have got far with that hole in your thigh –
turns out I was wrong. And, just to be difficult
you managed to fall where we couldn't find you.
How did you know where I was? she asked.
Followed my nose – you stink Numeh.

She dug her nails hard into his arm.
Ow! Stop that, you ungrateful shrew!
he pulled her hand away from his face –
*I've been looking all night, trust you to get trapped
in a crack between boulders – I heard you crying.*
She tensed – *I wasn't crying –*
                                        *Crying-
moaning – groaning – Oh, and grunting –
like a knackered old caribou in labour.*

The camp appeared.
                        Karrik was killed,
Ma'khen said – the words too taught,
too loud. Numeh gasped. He nudged her,
Keep going. I can't talk about it.

                            *

Numeh's wound was healing and though
it took too long for her, she held
her tongue when they said she should rest,
sit on the sled with the weak and young.

Whenever she could she listened carefully
to the women and children captured
after the attack, as they talked softly
to each other in their own language.
Sometimes she'd say a word in hers –
the name of an animal, the food they ate –
or make the girls giggle with a silly game.

One morning the baby boy's mother came over,
and started to speak, not asking if Numeh
understood - face ugly with fury,
then pinched with pain at what had happened

to her tribe. Numeh watched words
leap from the woman's lips, lunge
towards her, bought alive by anguish –
violent sounds spitting like snakes,
weighted with a suffering so huge
Numeh saw deer gralloched - guts spread -
flies crawling - felt vultures cram their heads
into her own belly, beaks burrowing in.
She wanted to make the woman shut up,
to keep her story to herself,
she had no choice but to hear it –
first sickness, a frightening new sickness
they couldn't cure. In days people died,
those who survived were weak – the wandering,
scavenging months, minds mad with hunger –
their children – limbs down to bone and skin,
too still, too frail to ask for food
or cry – the little bodies carried
for days, held close by mothers who couldn't
look into empty eyes in dead faces –
stumbling across the camp – the attack –
their men weeping as they hid them in bushes,
took their young sons to be slaughtered –
how she'd muffled the baby's mewling,
felt her hands press harder on its face,
its cry growing faint, drifting further away,
a ghost baby now – no pain, no hunger –
the bush yanked aside – the baby yelling.

Each day Numeh taught the women
and girls one word her own tribe used.
In the year it took for them
to find somewhere to stay the four
could speak Hegantii, the baby boy
knew the words for *mother, father*

and *kiss,* though they often chose
to use their own words between themselves.
There were some who said they should stop,
now they were part of the Hegantii tribe,
others maintained it mattered that
they knew who they are, where they
had come from, who their people were.

*

The place the Hegantii chose to call home
was more water than land – lakes
streams and pools were strung like beads
across the land – soil had an old smell –
something they all thought they knew –
a cold thing? a blood thing?
a thing of salt? No-one could name it.

They saw no villages, no signs
that it was home to any tribe –
a few burned spots from small fires where
people travelled through in summer.
Its wetness seemed to be why no-one
lived there, but they were water people,
half of their lost world was ocean –
Now there were no whales, no sea,
no seals, all water was a comfort.

*

I've always known.
                        Numeh stared
at Ma'khen – *No, you never, you liar –*
you fucking didn't know – no-one
knew. She made a grab for the garments

scattered round them. *No-one knew!*
she yelled, *you're lying Ma'khen.*

When we were small, he started, *you were
different – not just your body – you –
could you calm down and listen for once.*
Numeh had stood up in shock,
*No-one's seen my body since
I was little. You all laughed
at me. It made me mad. And
ashamed. You made me weak with shame –
I couldn't fight the feeling off.
Anger made me strong again,*
she scowled. *Strong enough at least
to beat the shit out of any of you.*
He sat in long grass looking at her.
I could now if I wanted, she said.
I've never laughed at you Numeh,
he said.
      Liar, she shouted back.
Once, he said. *I did it once!
I laughed because you looked like
a duck pecking at its own arse –
it was funny – that was why I laughed,
not because your body was wrong,
I've always thought your body is beautiful.*
She glared. *You never saw it, no-one
saw it once I was old enough
to take care of myself – no-one –
'til I decided to let you touch me.*

Ma'khen shook his head. *When the spirits
sent you out to sit on the shore
watching the ocean for three full moons
so you could warn when danger came,*

*I was the one who helped your mother
feed you, wash you, change your clothes.*

My mother did all that, not you,
she snapped. *You never saw my body
'til I was injured in the attack
and you decided to cut my clothes off,
ruined them for no good reason.*

He laughed. *Have it your own way woman.
You will no matter what, won't you.*
He rolled towards her, touched her thigh
where the spear-wound scar shone pale.
Is that what I am, a woman? she demanded.
He kissed the place pierced by the blade.
You don't need me to tell you Numeh.
She took hold of his hair and pulled
his head back, *Look at me!* she shouted.
*Does this look like a woman to you?
This hair all over me? And this –
this lump here – in my groin – like
a bollock that hasn't dropped – this
cunt where everything's wrong –
is this going to give you babies? –*
her hands had loosened in his hair.

*I don't know – it might – I've never
thought about it if I'm honest.
Do you want babies, is that why
this pains you so much?* He stared.
*Of course you do, how dim of me
not to see that. You've always said
you were a girl, why wouldn't you want
babies?* He touched the scar softly.
How selfish I am – I'm sorry Numeh,

really sorry, I should have realized.

He got to his feet. *I don't have answers,
I don't even know if there are answers
but we both know what we like –
whatever you say and whatever you feel
about your body, it makes me ache
when I think of it, when I remember
all the things we can do to each other.
That's been enough, everything
I wanted. I wasn't thinking of what else
you might want.* A moment later
Numeh had flicked his feet from under him,
pinned him firmly. *I don't just fuck you
for the babies though, my friend.*

*

    *whenever I think of how things were when I was growing up
    I think of shame   I know I'm not remembering
    the shame itself only what I did to keep it away*

    *I wanted to be like everyone else
    I remember hiding   I was very good at it
    covering my body   creeping off to swim alone
    the fear that they might follow me   try to catch me out
    not letting my own mother see me without my clothes*

    I remember   but I don't

    *then it's back   like a punch I didn't see coming
    and I'm burning hot   my face is on fire
    a bloated red thing
    all the ugly wrongness of my
    of my*

body
blisters and swells
until I know my skin is going burst

the first year we arrived we didn't name the place although
the spirits told the shamans we should stay   instead we made
a temporary camp   watched for bands of summer hunters
coming through   every time our scouts saw them approaching us
we made signs that we were here   went out with gifts to meet them
there were a handful of small groups   they were keen to trade
food and tools   then later they came with lovely things of copper
and they had nothing like our woven fabrics in their tribe

that summer the place began to grow into out bones
not home   not yet
but we saw it bloom   we fished its lakes   we breathed it in
when wind and water let light settle
the small shut places
of our hearts cracked open

summers were warmer here it made us go a bit giddy
people played with children   some of them swam   not me of course
not while anyone was near   I had a secret spot   a deep
earthy pool hidden by bushes   when I took off my clothes
slipped into its chill   swam down
all the slab and bulk of my ugly body disappeared
everything   everyone   every thought was gone and I
moved through water – moved like water – in water
my body
weighed the same as light

that second year was my sixteenth   we found ourselves laughing
quietly at first for fear of strangers hearing us
then out loud   we talked of a name for our new home
after the years of fear   of running and searching

after that long walk when we left Hahg-ha-whe we felt safe

*although my little pool was very deep I taught myself
how to control my breath so I could dive down long enough
to touch the silty bottom   in my pool I could dart
and turn faster than fry   the heft of my heavy body
was gone   I was a fish-girl made of water and light*

It was a time of grief, a time
of making, of growing and of peace.
Stillness settled round them. The stories
they told were of sea and seals,
a far shore, their tribe's long travels,
of how they learned language
when the world was new.
                            Numeh
cherished and carried the words. Gradually
the land was becoming a part of them
and they felt themselves a part of that land.

*

Numeh's skin was stretched and yellow
as the golden-rod growing everywhere –
even the whites of her eyes were yellow,
she shimmered with yellowness.

Her back hurt – she tried to turn,
pain stopped her. She couldn't eat,
food and water made her heave.
Ma'khen was sitting at her side
when the boy's tall frame blocked
the daylight flooding through the doorway.
How are you Mama?
                     I'm happy son.

She smiled at his sudden laugh.
*Why is that funny – why wouldn't I
be happy?*
        *Is your back bad Ma –
do you want dad and me to move you?
Not yet Setiniq, I want to feel the sun –
we named you for the sun and now
you're making shadows over me.*
He stepped quickly to the side.
Stop teasing him, Ma'khen said.

The two of them sat by her bed
in the bright oblong of light –
the air was still and summer warm –
Setiniq hummed softly to himself.
What's that song? she wanted to know.
You used to sing it when I was small,
he said – *Seal Song – you called it.
Seal Song – I remember,* she said.
*We made it up, your dad and me.
You loved the little seal-woman so much
we made that song for you. Do you
still have her?*
        Of course, he said.

Light arced slowly across the floor
until it shone full in her face –
soft and kind, it kissed her skin.

She knew that in the shadowy corners
of their hut, grief hovered – gone things –
lost people – home – loved land –
the spaces left by every loss
were waiting to wrap themselves around
Ma'khen and the boy – death drew grief

towards it – called it closer in the night –
she knew it waited in water, tree,
song – that loss would sometimes squeeze
the breath from them both when fire flickered
or a certain birds called. She thought of Karrik
and grandmother Umma, of the unruly ocean
the tribe would know in tales but never
see again.
        She sighed quietly
to herself and shut her eyes.
Are you alright Numeh – anything you want?
Ma'khen asked. She opened one eye,
looked at her husband and their son –
No...nothing...nothing at all,
she said.

*

Cloud

      I *am*

          Ke-teh-ha

I am old

      in my head   *in my*

head   *I hold*

the

in my

        head I hold

the story the names

    of the an   *the an*   *the ancestors for our children*

in

    my head

      I

        am Ke-teh-ha I am

old

I am

    keeper of

      the stories

When the world began the tribe lived on an island in the middle of the sea. They spoke only as animals speak, they had no name and couldn't understand the words of the Great Spirit. The Great Spirit said to Wind, "You are strong, you must blow language over the people so they can hear me and know their name." So Wind blew and blew but he couldn't blow language over them. Then the Great Spirit said to Water, "You are powerful, you must wash language to the people so they can hear me and know their name." Water flooded and flowed but she couldn't wash language to the people and they couldn't speak and had no name.

The Great Spirit saw that neither Wind's strength nor Water's power could bring language to the tribe so he gave them a child – a daughter called Qischaq, gave her the gift of language. She carried it to the people and they understood language and spoke and named themselves Hegantii.

When he saw that the people could talk, the Great Spirit told Qischaq she must carry new words, sacred words. that would guide and teach the people the ways of the spirits and the ways of the world. But the words of the sacred language were heavy as a mountain – Qischaq tried to carry them in her arms but she couldn't lift them. She tried to carry them on her back but they dragged her to the ground. She begged the Great Spirit for help to hold the words safe – she was only a child and the weight of the words was too much. The Great Spirit said the gift was hers and she must bear it alone, she must take it to the tribe and she must keep the words safe for all time. So Qischaq collected up the words again and filled her heart, her head, her mouth and her belly with them, she filled baskets and buffalo skins with them and balanced them on her head, then she made the long journey and took the new words to the tribe.

*

She was born into the black of a night
with no moon and cloud covering
the stars so they called her Ke-teh-ha.

From birth the sun was not a friend –
day-heat weighted too heavy on her,
day-sky was too close, too low,
the air of that place was the wrong air
and though she loved the lake like a sister,
its water was thin, the taste of it
was leaf small. To Ke-teh-ha it seemed
that the Great Spirit had forgotten something
when he made the air and water.

Tim after time she asked grandfather
what the Great Spirit had got wrong.
Grandfather said that the Great Spirit
knew everything, made everything perfect,
told the girl that as she grew
she'd dream a dream that would answer

all her questions. She prayed quietly
and alone, asked Bird Spirit to send
a dream of air – asked Stone Spirit
to send a dream of earth – she asked
Fish Spirit for a dream of water.

Every night she dreamed, in each dream
she was running. Someone was running
beside her – from the foot-fall and breathing
she knew it was a woman – day blistered –
in the distance land was darkening –
she tried to speak – her mouth stayed shut –
when she tried to turn to see the runner
her eyes were held by the horizon –
her mother was calling her to come home
but she couldn't stop, couldn't go back.

They ran on through the dream. Pines ragged
the skyline. At twilight she turned and saw
the face of the woman running with her –
saw the face that her own tribe wore,
saw her father, saw her mother
who was the keeper of False Face,
saw the face she saw in summer
when the lake returned her own face to her.

She stretched her hand to touch the shoulder
of the woman who ran beside her,
skin wet with the sweat of running,
lifted her fingers to her lips,
tasted water – tasted salt.

Ke-teh-ha woke, turned towards
the rising sun, away from rivers,
from leaf-thin lakes, from the land

the buffalo shaped and began to walk.

*

I

am

Ke-teh-ha in my   in   my

        I keep the   hold the

something   in my head isn't

       I   am

      old   I   am old

I   am

the names

     the story

Qischaq grew taller and stronger, she carried the words, kept them safe, but still they grew heavier. Too often they slipped from her arms or fell from her head, she had to gather them up again and again until she was exhausted. When she asked the Great Spirit to stop the *words getting heavier, the Great Spirit said Qischaq must learn to carry them herself no matter how heavy they were so she cut off her long hair, plaited strong ropes and a net to hold the sacred words and a harness to wear. When they were finished, she put the words in the net, put the harness on, got down on her hands and knees and crawled over the ground, dragging the words behind her to keep them safe. In time she forgot what the words were like – forgot how beautiful they were – forgot the song they sang – knew only their terrible weight.*

Slowly, slowly the ropes wore thin, the harness frayed, the net began to strain. One day the weight was so huge that Qischaq's net burst wide open and the precious words were scattered across the world. She cried alone until her tears formed a stream that ran into the sea. The sea tasted Qischaq's tears – it had never known such sadness and its heart was filled with pity and tenderness. It promised the girl it would always love her and because Qischaq was alone the sea sent a gray seal to keep her company. Qischaq loved the seal and took him for her husband. When their children, Bri-ah and Brendn were born the sea loved Qischaq even more.

*

When day-heat was spiteful Ke-teh-ha hid,
walked when the sun was near the horizon,
searched the maps of bark and moss,
followed bird-paths and sky-patterns.
She could feel her feet touch earth
yet there were times when she seemed
to move through the land like vapour.

Season after season she listened for the sound
of other people, for someone to speak
so she would know she wasn't alone.
No voice came. Now and then she saw
a whisp of white smoke from far away,

thought of those people planting, trapping,
talking together as they worked,
singing, as her people sang.
She burned to find them but she was frightened
to come close enough to strangers
to hear them speak. When she lay down
to snatch at sleep, she thought she heard
a woman humming to herself –
a tender, lilting little tune.
Countless times she tried to find her,
opened her eyes, stood up and searched,
but there was no-one, only a bird
so high that she could hardly see it –
and all around, in all directions
swollen silence clotted the air
so she couldn't breathe, couldn't sleep.

Exhaustion caused her feet to falter,
filled her head with faces floating,
mouthing things she couldn't make out –
grinning, gurning, giggling at her –
couldn't sleep for strangers speaking
but never making any noise.

Her mother was walking towards Ke-teh-ha –
She reached her side, smiled and kissed her,
lifted her like a baby, wrapped her
tightly, covered her ears and eyes,
said she'd carry her child back home.
Ke-teh-ha cried, felt herself fall
into a sleep she couldn't wake from,
her mother taking her home and singing –

Shush child, I can hold you, carry you
Shush child, I can hold you, carry you

Honey-sweet sleep dragged her deeper,
her mother's song grew sweeter still,
saying she should carve a False Face,
listen to Lo-hadi who
would take her to a living tree –
told her she must carve her False Face,
carve it in the cool of morning,
carve its eyes as deep as canyons,
carve its nose as bent as corn stalks
when the buffalo trampled by –
said if she did, False Face would help her,
she'd never be alone again.

The soothing mother-song continued –
Ke-teh-ha drowsed, her desperate
loneliness waned in mother-warmth,
mother-voice, mother-love –
above all else she wanted to stay there
safe and warm but she was starting
to feel too hot, her body began
to sweat – she struggled – the skins tightened –
she begged her mother to let them loosen –
they tightened again and the mother-song
began to boom – Ke-teh-ha couldn't
hear her own voice over the violence
of the mother-song – in terror she tore
at the wrappings, reached to touch
her mother's face, fingers trying
to find the features Ke-teh-ha knew
better than her own – the curve of cheek
and brow, her mother's mouth.
                              Instead
she felt the beak of a colossal bird,
opening and closing – opening and closing –
the mother-song, the mother-voice

resounded round and round her head –
she stared into a glaring gray eye
in a gray feathered face and in
the dream she knew the mother-bird
had tried to trick her, make her do
a thing that would enrage the spirits,
so they would stop her, send her home.

When she woke on cold hard stones
the silence and the vault of sky-space
was too much.   She started to think –
maybe she should make a False Face
to heal the sickness in her heart –
told herself her people loved her
wouldn't want to see her suffering
all alone. But she knew False Face
was the healer for their whole tribe –
that no matter how much she longed
for comfort she could not claim False Face
for herself – she'd have to journey
on alone until she understood
what the Great Spirit had got wrong.

*

After the dream a dark cloud came
and settled inside Ke-teh-ha – she tried
to walk but her feet didn't want
to take her – tried to eat but her throat
clamped shut so she couldn't swallow –
the cloud thickened – she closed her eyes,
stood still.   Heavy rain fell round her –
day after day the world was deluged –

water washing, rivers running –
all living animals left that land.

On the fourth day it finally stopped.
On the fifth day Ke-teh-ha opened her eyes
and saw the land was little islands.
On the sixth day the islands spread wider,
on the seventh day only one stream remained,
purling past her. She sat and stared
at sticks and twigs swirling round stones,
listened to the sound it made –
leaf small, like the lakes of home –
and the storm cloud in her stomach shifted.

A bit of wood bobbed by. She watched –
it reached a rock, bumped and twisted –
she saw a mark – a cut? – a crack? –
a mouth? It turned again, the mark moved,
a sharp voice shrieked, *Get a move on girl!*
Ke-teh-ha was so shocked she couldn't
do anything and it floated away,
but the vehement voice bellowed back,
*I'm stuck! I'm stuck! Don't stand staring,
pick me up, you lazy lump!*
She chased along the stream after it,
its mouth screaming insults and instructions,
until it was caught in a tangle of twigs
and the mouth sounds were no more
than muffled moans and angry grunts.
She snapped some of the twigs trapping it,
to pull it free. The furious mouth
kept complaining – she was careless, clumsy,
too slow, too hasty. Ke-teh-ha tried
not to tug too hard at it,
to ease it gently, while the mouth grumbled on.

Even when it was loose and she lifted it,
the wood wasn't satisfied – *Why are you staring?*
it demanded. She couldn't stop herself saying,
You....you....you don't have a face.
The mouth shut, lips a thin line
as if it was trying to control itself,
then it hissed at her, *Don't have a face?*
Whose fault is it if I don't have a face?
Did you make your own face? No!
Make me a face girl, make me a face.

Cautiously Ke-teh-ha started carving –
ears first – the mouth said she was
too slow, too rough, she cut too deep –
when she asked if she should stop
the wood called her, *Silly child,*
told her to work faster, take more care.
Then a nose – Ke-teh-ha made it neat,
made sure it was straight. The mouth
was shouting less, letting her work on
uninterrupted until she finished
carving the pair of closed eyes.
When she set the wood down on a stone
the eyes opened, glared out at her –
Don't stand gawping, say something, it snapped.
Who are you? Ke-teh-ha whispered.
The wood was furious. *Look what you've done –*
carved my ears all wrong, carved
my nose too long, my eyes too small –
you haven't told me who you are
and now you want to know who I am!

Ke-teh-ha didn't know what to do,
she thought of running off, leaving it –
Don't you dare, the wood warned,

you carved me badly, you didn't care.

Ke-teh-ha knew she hadn't carved it
skillfully but she'd tried her best
and she was sorry. It ceased complaining,
thanked Ke-teh-ha for carving it a face,
said it had no name, said she
should name it. Ke-teh-ha knew at once
what name to give it – *Tu' Teh*, she said,
your name is Tu' Teh – wood friend.

Tu' Teh's eyes filled with tears –
she picked it up, sang a small song
of lake and family and buffalo.
Tu' Teh listened, promised to
advise her, help her for as long as
Ke-teh-ha needed, said it would
show her who she was and how
her people came to call the land
of many lakes they lived in – *Home.*

Through all the winters of her walking
Tu' Teh spoke to Ke-teh-ha of Qischaq,
daughter of the Wind and Water –
people, names poured from Tu' Teh to her –
terrible things – other worlds – wild wanderings.
A cloud of ancestors clustered close
talking - talking - reaching their arms out -
telling Ke-teh-ha to keep the stories
safe for their people. She grew terribly tired,
shouted at Tu' Teh to shut them up,
swore she'd throw Tu' Teh in scrub
for foxes to piss on if they all kept yapping,
said she'd turn round and take herself home.

Tu' Teh took no notice of her,
told the stories over and over,
sang songs from a different time,
strange sounds and notes that never went
where Ke-teh-ha thought they should,
though they seemed to seep inside her
calling up hazy, half remembered things.

The salt dream of the running woman
was more than memory to Ke-teh-ha,
it was the map she followed to find the thing
the Great Spirit forgot. She felt it
in the rhythm and ritual of walking,
saw it in mist and morning cloud
lifting like a spirit soaring,
heard it in the voice of Tu' Teh
in the high calls of gray geese.

Loneliness and loss were always with her
but greater than the desire to go back
was the urge to see what was ahead,
to find out what the Great Spirit got wrong.

*

I am

Ke-teh-ha mother of   *grand*

mother of

my mother was   *my mother was*

       say

    the name

my mother was my mother was my mother was

      in my h

        in my h

something

        in my head

  isn't right   *I am*

   Ke-teh-ha mother of

    the story

On another island lived a great bird who was strong and handsome but very vain. He called himself King of the Island. When he flew up, he could see that his island was small but the sea was huge. Then he wanted to be King of the Sea. He saw how much the ocean loved Qischaq and her children, saw that their island was bigger than his. It made him jealous and angry and he wanted to punish them. He ate all up the poisonous plants and all the venomous animals of the world, then it swallowed the sea. When its huge belly with filled with water it spread its immense wings, flew above Qischaq and her children and *all the tribe and hurled water at them until crops rotted and they were starving. When they were helpless with hunger it shit all the poison in its gut over their island so that the land and the people were very sick.*

The Great Spirit saw what the bird had done and told Qischaq to take the tribe far away over the ocean, away from the poisoned land but they were too frightened to leave – they begged Qischaq to stop the sickness with her songs and prayers so they could live for all time in their land but the words were poisoned by the bird – they had lost their power and the people were dying. The Great Spirit was filled with sadness to see their suffering so he gave a gift to Qischaq's daughter Bri-ah – gave her the of skill of swift and swallow to find their way across the oceans – gave Brendn the strength and wisdom to help her steer the tribe, safely to another land.

*

Years fell among ferns, lightened
like bones behind her. There were times
when she was small as a squirrel, a snail,
an ant, small as a single speck
of dust floating, frightened. Tu' Teh
chattered and scolded and told its tales
until Ke-the-ha came back.

                          Air began
to sing other songs, older songs
whose words were only the whispering
of dead grasses from a different land.
Sky-weight lifted as she walked east.

*

Without warning the world stopped – impossible
water swelled, wild and wide

towards the sun-rise. Ke-teh-ha stood
mesmerized by its sway – its surface
wasn't like the lakes she'd left,
it was a membrane holding in pure power –
this water was troubled by its own vastness –
a blue disturbance rolling – dark
and kind. She knelt on cold gray pebbles,
tasted water – tasted salt.

The ocean's slow repeated shush
was the breath of the running woman.
Here, sky did not press heavy on her –
air streamed – perfect as the Great Spirit
made it – perfect as grandfather promised.

She walked into the waiting ocean,
sank her body below the surface
and drifted, looking up at light,
face fragmented to shimmering angles
by light, eyes open in water, in light.

When she stood on the shore salt bloomed
to white paths that patterned her skin.
She saw now that the Great Spirit
had made the world as the world must be –
put buffalo, beetles, pine trees, squirrels
where they should live – air wasn't wrong,
the lake wasn't wrong. She wondered why
she'd felt a stranger on its shores,
felt alone when all her family
loved her dearly – her people held her
close and safe. The sea churned on.

*

Ke-teh-ha stayed there through the spring,
learning to let the salt sea hold her,
learning the ways of ocean, listening
to wave wash, seal song and whale call.
Sometimes she heard her mother shouting,
calling to her to come home,
but the sea said, *Stay Ke-the-ha –*
this is home, stay here, stay here.
She asked Tu' Teh what she should do,
Tu' Teh said nothing, so she stayed.

And slowly she forgot her family,
forgot the lake, forgot the land
where she was born, even began
to forget her mother's face –
it was as if the immeasurable sea
had cast a spell, stopped her remembering
who her tribe, her family were
and though she tried to find them they were
whisps of cloud in a restless wind.

One moonless night her mother came to her –
lake and leaf of home came to her –
family and flower of home came to her –
then, in her mind, she walked high mountains,
crossed river and plain, ran on through forests,
in an eyelid's blink – each step
carried her closer to her people,
to her dear, dear people.
                        The vision vanished
so suddenly it made her moan.

Tu' Teh spoke – Ke-the-ha couldn't
go home – the story wasn't a stone
thrown in a lake and sunk without trace,

it was circles spreading on the surface –
the crystals of salt on Ke-teh-ha's skin
mapped the route of the rest of her journey,
north towards a colder country.

Days ripened. Sometimes she swam –
when cloud lowered itself to the land
she walked. When winter roared around her,
and frost keened leaf to knife-blade,
she found food. Soon came snow clouds,
blizzards blasted, she dug a den
and curled up like a bear cub inside.

*

Earth was softening when Tu' Teh said,
Here – we're here Ke-teh-ha – listen –
She stood in silence, heard the air
from an older place spill open,
looked around her at the land,
saw the stones were laid in circles –
here were relics – the lost remains
of huts, a hearth, some bits of pot –
voices whose words she couldn't catch.
She saw faces, two together,
the same but not the same, both smiling.

Air was listless with the ache of loss –
those tumbled stones, no longer hoped –
they were more dead than anything
she'd ever known. Now she understood
what Tu' Teh meant by 'memory.'

She tried to recall her mother's touch,
her father's face, grandfather's stories,

the names of the ancestors – forced her thoughts
back to the tribe, but they had become
something she'd seen too long ago.
She cried out– stone swallowed her voice.

Tu' Teh said she was the keeper
of the words, the names, the stories
that bound her tribe to the world before,
the world she walked and the world to come –
said that she could not return
to her own tribe until she'd found
Qischaq's bones and brought them back
to Hahg-ha-whe, to her children.

Ke-teh-ha searched the shore and forests –
found the faces of her family
in grass that swayed like grass remembered
but never found Qischaq's bones.

*

    I   *am*

       in my h

       in my h

in my

hawk

I hold the

something   *in my*

something in

say the names

I am

afraid

of the black falling

I   am   falling

into

the story

For long years the gray bird hounded the tribe across the icy ocean. Whenever Bri-ah tried to stop he plucked a feather from a wandering albatross and touched her so she had to keep going. Slowly Bri-ah lost hope that they would ever find a place to make their home and her weary heart grew hard with anger for her mother who wouldn't share her strength and wisdom.

When the bird had chased the tribe onto a distant shore he decided they had travelled far enough from their island and sent a thick fog to hide everything so they would never be able to find their way home.

In that new land there were evil spirits – they saw that Bri-ah's heart was full of anger and her mind was hurt and they told her she must send Qischaq away. Bri-ah only wanted one thing – forgiveness from her mother. She couldn't find the words that would bring her mother's love back to her, she had no strength left to fight and she did the thing the evil spirits said.

Qischaq made herself into a pool of water but Bri-ah didn't drink from it. She became a ribbon of fog and tried to slip into Bri-ah's sleep so she could tell her daughter how she loved her, had turned her back because she loved her, so the tribe would listen when Bri-ah spoke. The evil spirits saw what Qischaq was doing – they knew they couldn't stop her and that Qischaq would speak to Bri-ah in her dreams so they tormented Bri-ah night and day so she couldn't sleep – wouldn't hear her mother, wouldn't knew what she had done out of love for her daughter.

When the Great Spirit came back and saw what had happened, he knew he had given too great a load to a child. He couldn't undo what the evil spirits had done, couldn't bring Qischaq back, couldn't mend Bri-ah's mind. He hid the precious words deep in the heart of the tribe so they would be there for all time and the people could live in peace.

*

Time wore Ke-teh-ha – hope thinned
to transparency, like winter leaves
on starving soil. Her last shred
of strength drained away and she
slumped to the stony ground
beneath the brittle, dead branches
of a great tree clinging to the ground,
crawled deep into the cold cavern
that was once pale rings repeating,
breathed in spore-stink, shut her eyes –
still the world was too much – too close.

*

Tu' Teh was speaking from somewhere else –
stand up   stand up   stand up   stand up
until the voice was part of the pattern
beating in Ke-teh-ha's brain.
stand up   stand up   stand up   stand up
so far away she could hardly hear it –
words slipped – sound was thought –
thought became a fervour of flies –
their buzz swelling, swarming, lifting,

circling above, three perfect circles,
in each an eye. The first eye gazed
with no pity– in the next
the dregs of the world were draining away –
the eye of the third was tightly closed –
she blew it softly, it opened slowly –
in it a gray stone smoothed by sea –
she stretched out, grasped it, opened her mouth,
lay it on her tongue – fell towards
into nothing.

*

Wind oozed through the hollow tree,
touched Ke-teh-ha with trembling fingers
soft as moths – Tu' Teh sang,
stand up   stand up   stand up   stand up
but Ke-teh-ha couldn't hear.

The wind grew louder, shook her shoulders,
blew icy breath over her body
but Ke-teh-ha couldn't feel.

Clouds massed. A sudden storm –
wind blasted, water loosened soil
until roots ripped from the earth.

Ke-teh-ha felt rain sting her face.

Beside her in the gash of ground
lay a pile of pebbles, a few shells and
a skeleton, curled up on its side,
arms wrapping ribs as if for comfort,
in its fingers a metal fragment,
one side patterned with a perfect arc

and in it a circle flecked with bright colour.
She wept for the little bones.

Tu' Teh said, *Stand up*. She stood,
looked down at the lonely bones,
gathered them gently with the scraps of metal,
the few flakes of turquoise and red,
took her ancestor to Hahg-ha-whe,
lay her with the bones that lay there.

Tu' Teh said she must leave her wood-friend –
lay it with Qischaq, so water and wind
and time would make them one and the same.

Ke-teh-ha couldn't bear the thought
of being alone again, of losing
her friend and helper, still she knew
Tu' Teh was right. Tears streamed
as she lay Tu' Teh among the leaves
and soil with Qischaq.
                    She couldn't let go.
Tu' Teh started to sing softly –
a little song they'd sung together
many times – still Ke-teh-ha clasped
Tu' Teh tightly in her hand.

Through that day Tu' Teh's voice faded
with the light – Ke-teh-ha let go,
gently scooped the soil in place,
knelt beside them through the night

Morning – not a sound – no bird-song,
no scuffling animals, no wind, no rain –
Ke-teh-ha didn't know if this
was death or dream or something else –

when she shouted out to Tu' Teh
there was no answer. Frantic now,
she scrabbled in the soil to find them –
all she found were the fragments of bone,
specks of bright colour, a bit of wood.

Seven days she watched waves curling,
waiting for the voice of Tu' Teh
to tell her off for her silly sulking,
tell her stories, sing to her –
no voice came.
               At the close of day
she heard a sound she'd heard before –
heard the woman who ran beside her –
heard her breathing through that night –
dreamed that they were running together,
side by side back to her home.

She dreamed on – as the sun came up
the breathing faltered, began to fade.

When she woke the sun had risen,
the breathing of the woman was gone.
She began the walk back to her tribe.

*

Ke-teh-ha lived life with her people,
where the sky weighed heavy on her,
where the water was leaf-small
and the air was always wrong.

All her years she tried to hold
the names and stories in her head
and though her brain began to cloud

she kept the words safe for her children
and all the children of the tribe.

In dreams she swam in different water –
a blue disturbance, dark and kind,
holding her body up like an offering –
tasting water, tasting salt.

*

I

am

Ke-teh-ha

I

am

the   story

*

Steam

Grace tried to conjure the creature
that looped up from earth, lifted air
into slow spirals – that seemed to be
made of sound but wasn't a sound –
that took dust and taught it to flow
like a river around rock – she'd caught
the stink of its breath but if there were words
for such a thing she didn't know them

> *world is tasting my skin   its snake-tongue flickers near my face*
> *now I lay me*
> *what's your name*
> *world is a gobbet of gray spit hoiked up on hard ground*
> *one   two   three   four   five   six*
> *chunks of hair   count them again*
> *get away from the window*
> *say your name*

She was squatting. Dry grass scratched
her legs. A beetle appeared between
her feet. She needed to pee – *don't pee* –
the little load of borrowed light
balanced on the beetle's wing-case
wobbled towards her toes. She tried

to wriggle them away – *don't pee* –
she needed to pee. The beetle stopped,
scurried back. She pee'd and pee'd –
drowned the beetle. There was no beetle.

When the nightdress was whipped away
she was small, unsteady. The dormitory
walls were lines of eyes watching
as they lifted the leather down from the door,
strapped the bare meat of her buttocks.
One Two Three Four
Five Six   for wetting the bed.
She was learning to count, learning too
that the strap would cleanse the savage from her.

*

Steam billowed. Blebs of scum
shawled each sheet, dragged it down
as she threw them in the boiler's thick,
gray water. Her sister said
they should steal the strap, whip the whites
to the laundry yard, light the fire
and when the water was bubbling hard
get the wash sticks and shove them all in
one by one, hold them under
until their faces bobbed back up
boiled and red. Her sister said
their people's words for *water* and *face*,
told silly stories that made Grace giggle,
spoke of their own gods, gave them names –
each name fell like a stone
thrown into a stream and sunk

> *black hair in clumps on the floor*
> *one   two   three   four   five   six*
>   *count them again   don't count them again*
> *world is a wasp   is a maggot in my mouth   chop chop chop*
>   *now I lay me chop chop chop*
>   *now I lay me what's your name girl*
>   *world is a maggot say your name*

Surely floor-boards should get thinner
with every scoured day? A silver-fish –
she watched its quick, beautiful body,
slapped her hand down hard, smeared
its gun-metal gleam across the wood,
picked the cloth from the caustic water
and wiped away all shimmering trace.

She scrubbed harder, saw the boards
wear to transparency – white faces
rushing in – a white hand reaching
for the strap – saw their shock
as the boards beneath their feet dissolved –
saw them scrabbling – the floor gulping
until there was not a trace of them.

                *

What was swallowed instead were years,
her voice, her sister's hot quick words,
mountains of hair, rows of marching
children – even the creature that taught
the dust to dance, slipped away
down the gaps between the boards.

Her sister was strong, spoke their own tongue –
they held her down, forced soap in her mouth –

she whispered the old words into the night,
told Grace how to make the sounds
for – *bird* and *home* – talked of the tribe –
told Grace tales of their before time –
called up pictures – their people fishing –
the mothers' tears when the children were taken.
But the pictures never belonged to Grace,
her sister was long gone and the leather strap
had taught her to keep her red mouth shut.

*

The train was sliding towards the horizon,
its noise and steam were almost gone
when she stepped down from the station platform.

There was too much sky here – it made
her dizzy – the ground felt thin – dangerous.
Behind her the tracks stretched back
to the school – she was walking towards
a different word whose sound was a swarm
of flies round meat – *Reservation*

> *keep moving   keep counting*

The path she was walking on felt old.
Rain fell – she tilted her face
to the terrible sky, held out her tongue,
tasted leaf, air, the heft of loneliness –
heard her sister's dead voice, her dead words.

She walked for weeks. Rain stopped. Earth steamed.
Away to the north lay astonishing water,
to the east she could see the settlement.

The sun was slipping into the brief gash
of sky-space between cloud and land –
the late light calling up boiler-house fires,
her burning buttocks, her sister's face,
lips like her own. She thought about
the silverfish and howled. The sound
was violent and hungry – a violation –
the way it rattled round her skull
scared her – she struggled to shut it out

> *now I lay me*
> *now I lay me*
> *now I lay me*
> *now I lay me*
> *now I lay me*
> *now I lay me*
> *now I lay me*
> *now I lay me*

She sank onto wet ground and slept.

And it was there! – not near enough
to see but she knew its sharp-sour smell –
the curve and the colour of it rising up.
It circled closer – watched her – whispered –
Open your mouth child – speak –
her jaws and teeth were wired together –
she tugged the twisted knots – blood oozed –
thickened to dark clots on her tongue –
Open your mouth child – speak –
She clawed at the choking mess till her lips
moved, opened her mouth but no sound
came and the creature was already gone.

Light on the horizon – her bones hurt.

She struggled to stand up – wet clothes
stuck to her body, chilled her skin

>*world is a dirty thief dirty bed-wetter gobbing and guzzling world*
>*should be beaten*
>*one   two   three   four   five   six*
>*for wetting the bed   chop chop chop chop clumps on the floor*
>   *world is a   world is a   world is a chop chop*
>   *get away from the window*
>*chop chop chop chop*
>*chop chop chop chop*
>*chop chop chop chop*
>   *what's your name*

Someone was walking the path towards her,
a woman. Her sister. Not her sister.
An old woman. They looked at each other.
The woman's eyes darted to face, dress,
boots, hair – back to her face –
she said a word then turned away,
walked the track the way she'd come.
Grace heard herself shout – *My name
is Grace.*
      The woman glanced back briefly,
said her own word once more – walked on.

*

No-one in all the towns she passed through
wanted to pay Grace to work –
there were things they wanted her to do,
dirty names picked out for people
like her – words – ready and waiting
in their mouths. But no money for
her kind.

        When she went to work
at the mine, wearing the boy's cloth cap,
jacket and trousers she'd stolen, her skin
smeared with coal dust to cover it up,
she was convinced the chute boss would
pick her out, throw her out,
sure the breaker boys would see
she was a girl, give her away.

The boss walked down the breaker line –
Grace shuddered so much she thought
he'd be bound to spot the shivering.

She bent over the juddering belt
sorting the lumps of slate from coal,
willing her body to stop shaking.

He noticed nothing. Relief rushed through her,
tears drew clean lines in the black dust
coating her face. He watched and walked –
up and down   up and down
pacing out her panic. Time turned
to coal on a conveyor belt –
relentless   repeated   moving on
staying the same. The pattern of it all
was almost a comfort – the chute boss passing
hundreds of hands like small machines
sorting and breaking   pain swamping her
the terrible noise rattling round
her head   pain   the chute boss passing
cold squeezing the blood back from
her frozen feet and fingers so that
each pulse of pain was welcome and dreaded
the chute boss coming towards her   her hands
making their mechanical movements

    the chute boss approaching
                    the chute boss behind her
    the chute boss approaching
                    the chute boss behind her
    the chute boss approaching
                    the chute boss   more pain
pain at the back of her head   more pain
the conveyor of coal swimming up
towards her face   her head snatched back
cap swiped off   spinning away
for the world to see what she was.
Lazy little shit! – you're not
paid to sit on your arse all day –
faster boy, or it's the boot for you –
his mouth was so close to her ear she smelled
his onion breath, half-expected
to feel his teeth sink into her flesh.

All she wanted in the world
was to get up, turn to him
and gob in his hard, grimy face.
She sat still, waited for him to work out
she wasn't a boy. And she wasn't white.

His punch between her shoulder blades
slammed every scrap of breath out of her.
He moved on. She got to her feet,
took a chunk of coal from the belt
and hurled it at his head. As her arm
arced forward the boy beside her jabbed
hard in her ribs – the coal shot sideways,
the sound as it struck the wooden post
and her angry shout were smothered by
the thunderous clatter of the conveyors.
He pinned her arms to her sides as someone

behind covered her mouth and hissed
Shut it! She couldn't work out what was happening –
her knees buckled – the boy next to her
on the bench mouthed, *Watch.*
                        She worked
and watched.
            Slowly the shed became
the boss – his slight lean to the left
the faint drag of his right foot
the slope of his shoulders   the way he hovered
behind a boy before he hit out
his eagle-eye fixed on a face
as he closed in for a crack across
the knuckles with his cudgel.
                        Counting
in her head was a kind of comfort

> *one   two   three   four*
> *one   two   three   four*
> *one   two   three   four*

Imagining where he was when she
couldn't see him made her feel sick
but it was better than not knowing.

Nine times his huge back heaved past her –
the boy nudged her, held up one finger –
ten – the hard face swam towards her

> *one   two   three   four*
> *one   two   three   four*
> *one   two   three   four*

it filled the world

one two three four
one two three four
one two three four

closing in

one two three four
one two three four
one two three four

behind her now

one two three four
one two three four
one two three four
one two three four
one two three four
one two three four
one two three four

coming closer

one two three four
one two three four

past again
the slab of his back
moving moving moving moving
shrinking towards the shed's far wall.

When it was almost at the end
the boy bent forward, slipped a broken
bit of board from beneath the bench
and wedged it in the conveyor chains.
Sound changed – gears grated then screamed –

the back became a furious face
mouthing obscenities, obliterated
by the busted machine and the boys' cheering.

There was still a smear of sunlight
between the buildings as they left.
If you'd have hit him, you'd be dead meat, girl.
The boys were walking on either side.
You got digs?
                She didn't answer,
kept her head down, hurried on.
She hasn't got digs Louie, look at her,
she's an Indian, she hasn't got digs.
Grace darted away down an alley –
they chased until they caught her up –
No need to run, none of us have digs.
we'll show you where we sleep,
it's no hotel but it's a heap safer
than the street. You don't want fellers
after your quim all night, do you?
It's warmer too, where we sleep.
Are you an Eskimo? the other boy asked.
Shut up Frank, Louie snapped.

                      *

There were two other girls she knew of
in the breaking shed. Neither spoke
and beneath the black dust she could see
that both of them were white.
Like her they kept their heads well down,
their bodies covered and kept quiet.

In front of Frank and next to Louie –
Grace sorted slate, broke coal, six days

a week, ten hours a day for two
full years. Her soft young bones began
to take on the shape of sorrow,
pain and fear. At night she prised
her fingers open, her spine straight.

They got hit, they got hurt –
too often, exhausted eyes lost focus,
coal became a thick, black blur
and the violent clank of the conveyor
was water or bird-song. Or a lullaby.
Boys died when that happened,
Grace had seen it – seen the scrap
of inconvenience a body became
once it stopped its work, or worse,
snagged the machine, where it must stay
until the shift was done and they dragged it free.
    Louie, Frank and Grace
watched each other for falling asleep –
at any sign of it, a sharp slap,
a poke, a punch would jolt them awake.

Fear turned out to be her friend –
always afraid of being found out
her mind was more alert, muscles
more ready to run if the boss clocked
her breasts or the curve of hips
underneath the baggy boy's clothes.
If he knew he didn't care –
she was as fast on the belt as the boys,
made less mistakes, caused less trouble,
didn't skive, kept her mouth shut.

One shift Louie lost concentration,

let his hand linger too long
near the clanking conveyor chain
and flesh and bone were ripped apart
and Frank and her were trying to wrenched him
unconscious, out from underneath it –
she couldn't stop herself from crying –
that was when the boss stared,
as if in the ten thousand times
he'd walked the line, he hadn't seen her.
As his hand reached out to take hold
of her shirt she sank her teeth
deep into his filthy flesh –
Frank mouthed, *Run,* and she was flying
past the chute boss – past the line – leaving
Frank and Louie – leaving the only
kindness she'd known since her sister vanished.

*

Scrubbing the steps and flags at the front
of the house was the worst job. Out there, on her hands
and knees, Grace knew that anyone passing
might poke her arse with a well-polished boot,
knock over the bucket, shout names, spit.
The second she turned her back to the street
the dormitory strap dangled over her head.
Some days her sister's face swam up
from the caustic water, mouth moving but making
no noise. In the house Grace moved like a ghost –
the servants complained that her silent skulking
put them in fear that their souls would be stolen.
The Mistress saw she was strong and quick,
didn't give any trouble, did all she was told,
said she could stay. So for a year
she blacked the boot-scraper, beat carpets, cleaned boots,

cleaned toilets, laid fires, scrubbed floors, emptied slops.

The servants said she was lying – she could speak –
they'd heard her at night casting her spells,
in a language that sounded like an animal howling,
like stones being broken, like somebody breathing
their last – said they could tell she was cursing
the house and all who lived in its walls.

When he dismissed her the Master held out
a small piece of paper, an inventory, he said,
of the items she'd broken or stolen since starting,
said he was willing to spare her from jail
but must hold back her wages to cover the cost,
said that the Mistress had considered her modesty
and kindly decided she was allowed to keep
her scullery-maid dress but must give back the shoes.

*

Whenever she could, Grace would wait in the rail yard
for the moment no track-man or hobo was watching,
slip under the freight car. Riding the rods
felt safer to her than finding that she was
trapped in a car with a man who might have
wicked thoughts about what he could do to a girl
freight hopping alone – it had happened before –
she was safer suspended on narrow steel beams
hanging for hours, trying to hold on,
wincing whenever the train gathered speed
and the track was rough and cars bucked and swayed
like the terrified steers she'd seen white-eyed with panic
when they picked up the trace of slaughter-house stench.

*

The sea was something she could not have imagined.
As soon as she set eyes on it
she wanted it. It seemed somehow solid
and liquid – its mass, an animal moving
slowly through a dream – the sound
of it a new language – an old language.
Its endlessness enchanted her.

On the quay a cowboy band played
"The Girl I Left Behind Me," as
two hundred horses fought for breath
in the hot, dense air below the deck.
Crowds cheered each animal loaded –
cheered for the Indians – louder for the cowboys –
loudest of all for Annie Oakley
and The Showman.

                    When the ship left New York
its movement scared her, made her sick –
the rancorous drone and rumble of engines
behind the bunk made her sick –
the rancid air in steerage made her sick.

Twelve days to cross they'd told her –
it took sixteen. They said the ship
would take them to a different country –
she stumbled down the gang-plank into
a land the same as the one she'd left.

'Buffalo Bill's Wild West Show'
was a huge machine steaming its way
round Great Britain from town to town,
unpacking itself, parading and prancing,
dressing up, performing, packing up, moving on.

She'd been given Show Indian clothes to wear
for her part in the performance – they made her
ridiculous. Sometimes she thought of her sister –
the dead sounds she had tried to teach
that didn't belong to Grace. Nothing
belonged to Grace. She belonged
to The Showman – to The Show.

*

Queen Victoria was very fat.
Grace was getting used to the voices
and the crush of England – she expected
The Great Exhibition to be exactly
like any show but the scale of this
took her breath away. The whole world
was jostling, eating, laughing – even
the poor, with their pockmarked skin,
ragged clothes and black, broken teeth
were everywhere.

          The Showman said
that this performance must be perfect,
all of them had to be practice their parts,
the powerful people watching were used
to the best of everything, they had to be
better than the best.

            The bellowing crowd
was so loud in the Big Top Grace trembled.
Her legs felt like she didn't know them,
she seemed to be doing her bit of the show
but the noise was numbing everything –
she slipped to the ground. Somebody grabbed her,
hoiked her up. She felt a fist in her back

and staggered forward. The parade was passing
the Great Queen – Grace felt herself fall again–
a woman stumbled – a baby bawled loudly –
the world gave a gasp then everything stopped.
Grace saw the Queen's frozen face looking at her,
mouth hanging open, eyes wide with surprise –
movement – a figure leaned low from a white horse,
snatched up her body, limp as wet laundry,
threw it over the saddle. Then noise like a train,
the crowd came to life, on its feet cheering
as Buffalo Bill leaped down, plucked the baby
from its papoose, passed it back to its mother.
Grace saw the Queen's frown fade but behind
the relief, there seemed to be a sort of absence –
she thought of the silver-fish.

*

The buffalo were being bedded down –
Grace gazed, not noticing the beasts
that frightened her when she first joined the show –
now she was scared The Showman would come
and kick her out. Someone was close,
standing beside her, speaking softly –
Lakota language – the sound of it slipping
into her like an idea – as if skin
were no barrier – as if she were cotton
soaking up words without understanding –
each strange sound became her bones –
its music was her nerve and muscle –
its breathed notes everything she knew
about loneliness. She looked at the boy,
took his hand, led him through

wagons and cages, away from the camp,
stopped where its lights no longer shone.

When she wiped the war-paint he wore
in the show from his cheeks, he was crying.
She cried too – a bleak, blubbering,
ugly noise rising up from her belly.
He stroked her arm, spoke again.
She wanted to speak but words wouldn't come.

The park was studded with stands of trees –
dim spaces away from guttering gas lamps.
The glass hall glittered – Grace thought of coal.
The boy was gathering branches, building
a frame, a small teepee shape –
she copied his quick, sure actions,
found ferns and grasses to cover gaps.
The sweet green smell of growing things
filled the teepee. They took off their costumes,
spread them on the earth. Eyes shut,
they lay, listened to wind in leaves.
She heard his breath slow, then her own,
felt the scents of his skin and the ferns
fill her with a kind of calm –
leaf sound slowed – breath began
to loop and lift, to spiral up
as if it no longer belonged to them –
his lips on her face, her neck, her mouth
were a moth thing, then a biting thing –
she bit back – when he cried out
she bit harder, pushed his shoulders
aside and down to the ground – her hips
slid over his and suddenly he
was pushing against her. She panicked at the pain
but some warm thing in her was starting

to open like petals – she pushed back
and he moved under her until
they found the rhythm of running animals –
skin   bone   sinew   blood –

The teepee dissolved into the trees
as they made their way towards the lights.

*

Pain came in a wave. She kept walking.
A woman spoke, she walked straight on.
Her feet made their particular patterns
on the swaying floor of the steaming train

> *one two three four five six turn*
> *one two three four five six turn*

Some of the women were sleeping, others
were leaning in, talking together.
The pain came back, gripping her gut

> *keep moving   keep counting*
> *   one two three four*
> *five six*
> *turn*
> *keep moving   keep counting*
> *keep moving   keep counting*

one woman was watching her –
she stared back, kept her mouth closed –
the breaker boss loomed in front of her –
stretched sideways and melted away

> *now I lay me*
> *now I lay me*
> *keep moving*
> *keep counting*
> *one   two   three   four*
> *one   two   three   four*
> *one   two   three   four*

pain –
a fist full, then a carriage full of pain –
she had to stop   squat down on the floor

> *Keep counting*
> *Keep counting*
> *one   two   three   four*
> *one   two   three   four*

pain –
they were touching her   holding her up
talking   touching   fingers pushing

> *now I lay me*   *now I lay me*
> *one   two   three*

pain –

> *one   two*

pain –
probing   gripping   eel-slip and flood
school ceilings singing with pain
conveyor belts of pain

> *one   two*

pain –

    one two

pain –

    one two

pain –

they were holding her   plundering recess
and sea-cave for a slither of glair –
pain   pain   pain   pain –
hauling out something waxy –   huge –
something open mouthed and made from pain.

*

The women were Lakota, not her tribe,
but they helped her, showed her how
to suckle the baby, clean it, carry it.

Grace was frightened of its greedy mouth,
its fluttering bird fingers horrified her.
When it bawled they put it to her breast,
she shuddered at the touch of it,
with its sucking and urgent wanting.
It was doing it now – whimpering in the dark

        gobbing and guzzling   tasting my skin
   dirty bed-wetter
     what's your name
  spit hoiked up on hard ground
chop chop chop chop
   black hair falling

> *black hair falling*
>   *what's your name girl*
>   *what's your name*

They made sure that she fed the child,
strapped it to her back for each show.
The papooses of babies were passed around
to be petted by people in the best seats.
They kissed him, called him darling child,
handed him back. His small face
was a stranger. She didn't know him.

*

The little boy swamped his mother's silence
with his chatter, heaped his questions
all around her. He'd place his hands
on her cheeks, turn her face to his,
humming one note, or he'd wriggle
his fingers into her mouth till he
could prise it open and peer inside.
Asking, asking – where was his father,
where did they come from before the Show,
who were their people, what was their story?
Where was her voice? Why couldn't she speak?
She'd set him down and walk away
but she never harmed the boy.

*

The show trundled on – the boy grew taller.
He was quick, clever, copied everyone –
the Rough Riders' rolling gait – Custer's
death scene – the Sharp Shooters showy poses –
the Indians' whoops when they attacked

the Deadwood Stage – their painted dances.
The paying crowds laughed and cheered.

She was not to cut his hair. The Showman
saw everything – saw the boy running
through the camp, his hair cropped
to stubble – sent for her, said she
was not to cut the child's hair –
he was part of the show, people paid
good money to see real red-skins –
she must not cut his hair again.

*

Spain, Italy, America again,
across the Atlantic, back to England.
When the tracks first leaned towards
the bay and the train began to follow
its long curve, there was no water,
only an ocean of sand, as though
the earth had been stripped to bare skin.
The train clanked on, took its own time.

A skirr of metal on metal – they stopped.
All the windows were down – a wheeze
of sulphureous steam – someone coughed –
then the cry of a bird. The boy
was talking, shaking her arm, saying,
Open your eyes Mama ... look.
She opened her eyes, saw that they
were balanced on a thread of thin girders
spanning blue space, tethered to the land
on either side by a single stitch.
A bird was wheeling into the sun,
white body barely visible until

its gray back tilted towards them.
Below, where everything had been sand,
conduits, pathways, channels had appeared,
gullies spilled with wild water,
roiling ropes of it raced in.
The bay became islands – islands sank
until there was only the swelling sea
and the sound of the bird. She felt
the air from an older place spill open –
there was something she almost knew –
a taste on the air? a scent? Something
reckless and old flickered then faded.

*

The show site was outside of town
in an odd hidden valley, its floor very flat
and almost a circle. On one side a ruin,
on two dark woods rose quiet as widows,
the fourth was a steep, treeless slope,
its surface ridged and rippled as if
it was trying to remember water.

The day was weighted down with heat
as she started to climb it – feet sliding at first
then finding the measure – her fingers
grabbing at scrubby grass – eyes fixed
on the spot right ahead of her. Step by step
she rose over the ribs of ground.
Behind her the boy was following.
Close to the summit now – sweat dried
in a sudden breeze – her body shivered.

At the top she straightened up –
the narrow land looked west, at its tip

the raw town they'd paraded through,
beyond it an island reached like a ribbon,
mirrored the curve of the coast. To the east
the great bay, seamed by the bridge,
was slender sand-islands, threaded with silver.

The boy was standing beside her, staring
at the Big Top below in the valley.
In the heat haze Show Indians were dancing –
not The Showman's dressed-up Ghost Dance
they performed twice a day – this time their bodies
were making slow circles, colours were rising,
chant's repeating, snatches of sound
drifting up, close enough to catch.

The boy was dancing too – his torso
weaving air – winding, unwinding –
arms painting the pictures her sister had tried
to get her to see. He made one sound –
like the little note he'd hum
as he forced baby fingers into her mouth,
searching for her voice, though this sound
was an animal leaping from his lips –
looping and flowing like water round rock –
he came closer – the silverfish darted

> *clumps of black hair falling*
> *falling*
> *chop chop chop chop*
> *filling the floor*
> *count them again girl*
> *one   two   three   four*
> *get away from the window*
> *what's your name*
> *what's your name girl*

say your name

When she touched him, he stopped, put his hand
on her cheek, turned her face to his,
she heard her sister's fierce, small voice
whispering out of the dormitory darkness –
heard herself say their peoples' word
for *bird* – saw the silver-fish scuttle,
watched it vanish. Together they walked
to the rough-neck town on a rocky coast,
tethered to the shore of a gray sea.

Mist

F*uck off   fuck off fuck off fuck off   fuck off Mr*
*   Ferguson   fuck off book*
*   fuck off reading scheme fuck off fuck off   fuck off*
fucking   learning support
        d
           r
                i
     b
sound it out sound it out   sound it out   sound it out
                  b
d r   i

sound it out Evie sound it out   sound it out

Right from reception words refuse
to do what Evie wants, they dance
and jump, jumble themselves up –
d   r   ib
sand-hoppers pinging about the page –
they're doing it now –
i r   r
 b   d   r r d b db   i –
she stares at the letters – they skitter away.
Evie feels the familiar nausea

swelling in her stomach – her head hurts –
sound it out   sound it out   sound it out   sound it out
she tries to find words in the frightening swirl.
Amelia Goose appears, grabbing letters,
placing them side by side on the page
but they won't stay still enough for Evie
to read them. *Again!* Amelia yells
and Evie forces herself to focus –
eyes sting – room slews sideways –
she knows what's going to happen soon–
Amelia can't stop it, her sad face gets smaller,
she's leaving Evie, flying and fading –
sound it out sound it out sound it out sound it out
b
         d
 i
                r

she spews over book   desk   floor,
wipes her mouth on her sweatshirt sleeve.

*

Mam's packing, cramming clothes, cutlery,
half a pack of Penguins, Evie's pot-dog
into the laundry bag. Black bin liners
slump in a pile Evie needs to navigate
to get inside the doorway.
                            She groans.
Where we going this time? The heap slides.
Marley Street, Mam says. Evie dumps
her school bag on top of the bin bags.
Amelia settles next to it, looks around
and shakes her head. *So sad, so sad,
poor girl,* sings Amelia Goose

and goes on gnawing a scrap of flesh.
Shut up Amelia, Evie snaps.
Mam scowls. *You can stop your goose shit!*
Amelia and Evie laugh and laugh.
Goose shit, goose shit, stop your goose shit,
sings Amelia, waving the bone like a baton.
Evie tries to shush her but she's laughing
so much and Amelia just won't stop.
*I haven't got patience for your pretend friend,
shift your bag,* Mam snaps. *You can see
I'm sorting things. Pass me that pan.*
It isn't ours, Evie points out
and tosses it over. Mam tries to push it
into the bulging bag. *You're ten Evie,
don't tell me what is and isn't ours,
I've paid for this thing fifty times
over the last twelve months – it's ours.*
Eight months Mam, we moved here in May.
Amelia Goose looks bored and begins
to unravel herself until there's hardly
anything left. Evie takes no notice.

Mam stops wrestling with the saucepan.
*We can do better than this – it'll be
an adventure – a new start somewhere else –
we'll get cushions – new duvet covers eh!*
Can I change school, Evie asks.
*Maybe have a bit of a break –
I could help you unpack, sort stuff out?*
Mam sniffs. *You can walk it from Marley Street
you lazy little bugger, you'll never learn
if you don't go to school.*

                Making sure
no-one found out where they were staying

was exhausting. Every day Evie invented
new stories, new routes, new excuses, new ways
to dodge nosy teachers or kids on the look out
for an easy target, the runt, the loser

> *chimpanzees hunt in gangs they gang up on monkeys and tear them
> to bits   fuck off Libby what's it got to do with you if I've only got
> one school shirt just fuck off   I'm so tired   if there's no-
> one in when I get back I'll have a sleep Mam's creepy boy-friend
> won't finish work til seven   why does she always go for
> creeps even his flat is creepy   a proper bedroom for Evie he
> said   only the proper bedroom's full of his shite I'm sick of waiting
> til they've gone to bed I'm sick of sleeping on the sofa I'm sick of his
> weird mates and his whining about how much I eat when I get up
> what I watch on telly   there used to be this guy who slept
> under shelves in Tesco's everyone knew about it   he never pinched
> stuff   if Libby Dukes sniffs and says Sure – it won't let you down
> once more I'll fucking punch her*

*

Mam's prattling on – she's got a glass
in one hand, strokes Evie's hair,
calls her, *my baby,* feeds her chocolate buttons.
And though she knows it's the vodka talking,
that soon it'll be   *sorry babe   sorry babe*
and tears and her having to comfort,
make herself smile when Mam says,
*tomorrow we'll get our gear together,
leave this shit-hole town, won't we babe –*
still Evie loves it. These are the times
she feels the thin ropes tethering her
to the ground tense and tighten down.
Course we will Mam, she'll say, *tomorrow.*
And Mam'll start mumbling until

she falls asleep and it's over again.

*

Three years since she left Juniors – three years,
one house, two flats and too many months
sleeping on the floor or the sofa at a mate
of Mam's or some man she's hooked up with,
till the Social got them somewhere to go.
Three years – the vile tang of vomit lingers,
but she can blank out Mr. Ferguson's face
and his stupid voice with the mist she makes
in her head – she can blank out books,
blank out school, her own thick brain,
Libby Jukes laughing, letters sliding.
And Mam – she needs to blank out Mam.

Evie waits, watches the water –
tide's coming in, covering scars,
flooding gullies, submerging sand.
She's thinking of Ginny Green Teeth again –
the drowned girl who died for love,
grown over with weeds, who haunts water,
drags kids down to the depths by their hair.
In the playground they tell each other
they've definitely seen her – she's in The Rezza,
she's down the Red River at the back of Tesco
she's in the park lake, lurking in reeds –
no-one ever says they've seen her
in the sea. Evie sees her –
swimming beside her beneath the waves,
green hair swirling, face full of sorrow –
sees herself holding Ginny close
warming the cold dead flesh with her body,
stopping the sobs of the sorrowing girl.

She takes out her phone, taps Camera –
an iPhone4 – *Don't ask*, Stu had said
when he came in from the club one night,
slipped it into her hand and stroked
her palm with a thumb, flickered his tongue
and Mam flew at him like a harpy
and they were packing their things again.
She studies her face in the screen.
The one staring back is older than her.
She breathes on the glass- the girl dissolves-
wipes it with her sleeve, swipes right,
checks the tide-tables –
                    10.1 –
her heart jumps at the height of it –
the familiar, thrilling rush of fear –
and knowing that soon the salt sting
will wash everything away.

Mam doesn't want her going in the water

> *what does she know about anything   price of vodka in Bargain Booze   how to talk shit   how to kid herself   hide the empties how to find enough cash to buy the next bottle and when she's properly   pissed how to babble on about 'family'   we'll go to the library together babe do one of those Ancestry UK things how Mam how are we going to do that   you don't even know where the fucking library is*
> *how are you going to stay sober enough to do it*
> *how will I read it*
> *how will I write it down*
> *I   can't   read*
> *I'm fourteen*
> *and*
> *I*
> *can't*

fucking
read

The phone vibrates. Voice mail. It'll be
Mam wanting something. She stuffs it
back in her bag, rummages round,
finds her cigs – Mam's cigs – lights up.
Smoke drifts towards the tide-line,
to the wind-farm then the faint island
squatting in the sea towards the west.

Everyone knows she's as thick as a brick
and Evie knows there's no family, just Mam
and her and the useless fuckers Mam finds
and drags back. And it's always going
to be different this time – *honest babe*
it will, we'll be a proper family.
She'll start organizing days out
and video nights with nachos and dips.
Evie used to get excited –
looked forward to the fun night in –
looked forward to the travelling fair –
the picnic – the promises – the trip to The Lights
that all turned into arguments
or cans of coke and a bag of crisps
in the far corner of some cheap pub,
or the nearest offy with an offer on.

Evie blows smoke towards the sky,
aches with the weight of Mam's need.
Sometimes she knows there's nothing at all
holding her to the earth – no history,
no snaps of grand-parents smiling out from her past,
no track she could trace back – her and Mam
are ghosts – from nowhere, going nowhere.

She used to ask about her dad,
about aunties, uncles, grand-parents
but there were never any answers
and things got worse whenever she did,
it didn't take long for her to learn
to keep her questions to herself,
stop wanting answers. Still she couldn't stop
thinking – in dreams she's always reaching
towards something she can't name
arms stretching   straining   straining
leaning towards it   then falling forward
without a sound   the word for it lost
the wanting melting away in mist.

*

Evie snips the cigarette,
stands and takes her school uniform off.
She never looks to see if someone's
watching – let them watch if they want.
No cozzy – Mam's chucked it out again,
or hidden it – that won't stop her,
she'll swim in her knickers, she's done it before.
What matters is being in the water –
walking forward, feeling cold clamp
feet – thighs – creep past her hips
then her chest –
    counting
         waiting
five six seven she's in
in the sand-suspending
      salt-stinging
sea
  she's in
      head

                              in
scalp stinging with the shock of cold
seaweed on skin   diving down
fingers feeling for sand at the bottom
breath held   world held
salt smarting in open eyes –

the place she's going

                  is edge-land –
water

        salt

                earth

                        air –

all of them   none of them

she floats   feels her heart-beat slow

sea holds her safe   she's nowhere   and nothing

sound it out Evie   *sound it out*   *sound it out*
sound it out Evie   *sound it out*   *sound it out*
sound it out Evie   *sound it out*   *sound it out*

Something splashing – coming closer –
someone shouting – *Get out Evie*
get out get out –
              Evie's eyes open,
she turns to the sound, to the shore –
Mam's in the water, arms waving,
feet stumbling on the stony margin,

mascara smudged, the ends of her hair
hanging wetly on her skinny shoulders.
For fucks sake mam, stay where you are,
I'm coming to get you, just stand still!

Mam's crying as Evie manoeuvres her
over rocks and pebbles to the sandy patch
by her school stuff. She sits her down,
lights a cig, takes a long drag
holds it out towards her mother.
Mam is hunched forward, her heavy hair
snagging on grit and bits of shell.

Evie watches – *What were you doing?*
I thought you were going to drown, Mam mumbles,
you know it scares the shit out of me.
She looks towards the tide and shudders.
And you were going to rescue me, right,
a woman who's can't swim a stroke?
Mam stubs out her cig, smudges
dark ash across a smooth, gray stone.

I can teach you, Evie says. Mam turns
away from her without an answer.
Evie forces a shoe on a wet foot.
Don't go babe, we can dry off here,
have another cig and a chat or summat.
Evie snorts, stuffs her foot
in the other shoe – *what's up, you're usually*
desperate for a drink by this time?
She glances sharply, shakes her head.
I haven't, I promise I haven't Evie,
cross my heart and hope to die.
Evie stomps her way back up the beach.
Mam scrambles up, steadies herself –

Wait. Where you going babe?
                    No answer.

*

School used to lurk like an animal –
an ambush predator, skulking, patient,
its belly low, biding its time –
but it's GCSEs this year so school
doesn't want Evie there, with her thick brain,
lowering their pass-rate – a gesture at getting her
back into class, enough to cover
themselves. Then they leave her alone.

Most of the time she stays in bed,
sleeps as much as she can, curled small,
palms pressing tightly together,
tucked between thighs, duvet twisted –
a cocoon, hot with her body and breath,
where she's neither one thing nor the other
and the tenderness of her own touch,
the huge need, the bud of her body,
the orgasm they all talked about at school,
the shock of it, are only another
sort of sadness

> *I used to think it would be like everyone said but it isn't like any of those things   it's like the sea   like diving under the surface and sinking down deeper into a kind of black emptiness and I don't want to go there because I know it's death   it's like how I imagine dying will be*

tap tap

tap tap

She sticks her headphones on, turns them up
when Mam taps timidly at the door

   what does she want like I'd want her in here gabbling on
   why can't she just piss off

tap tap

tap tap

tap tap

tap tap   tap tap

   if she'd boot the bedroom door down kick it clean off its hinges
   send it spinning in splinters scream at me punch me I
   think I could stand it

tap tap
tap tap
tap tap

tap tap
Evie's back teeth grind – the grating,
the pressure, the screech, the sudden pain
in her jaw bone is a blessing that blocks out
every thing.
   Evie, open the door –
tap tap

tap tap
There's a crunch- a cracking noise
to one of Evie's big back teeth
so loud she stops –
                    and anger explodes –
Shut the fuck up and leave me alone!

Silence. Evie knows she's still there,
knows she'll be biting her bottom lip,
twisting that daft fake diamond ring
the last, lying boyfriend gave her –

tap tap

Please – open the door – it's Mam –

And it's gone – all that anger –
gone – and her heart huge with guilt
and pity and love. She turns the key,
goes back to bed. When Mam gets in
Evie kisses her wet cheek once –
Go to sleep Mam.

                    *

Someone's watching.
                    Evie swims
up the north end now. Since the sea
washed the track away and the council wouldn't
repair it again, there's just a few fishermen
and dog walkers who find their way
this far from the car park and no chance
of Mam making it here from the club.
An insect, some sort of hoverfly, settles
 on her purple polyester BJ Bargains

tee-shirt – a striped dot, suddenly still,
as if aware it's made a mistake,
made itself too visible, too vulnerable.
She prods a part-buried razor shell
with a finger, flicks the full length of it
out. It's a whole one, two halves hinged,
like a book always open on the same page.
She shudders.
                The Watcher's been here before –
more than once – older, ordinary,
alone, no dog, his steps slow
but not aimless, stopping to bend down,
turning over bladder-wrack on the tide-line,
crouching to look closely at things.

He hasn't looked at her but she knows
he's watching. She's not scared of him.

Silver sea holly is starting to flower
at the base of the dunes behind her.
The way it blues the air above
is something she waits for ever since
she first saw it and heard her own gasp
of amazement. It's going to do it again –
like it's leaning into its near future,
straining for the few seconds
when the sun's angle and cloud's absence
will coincide with its burst of blue bloom
and it stains the air for miles around.
She'll probably miss it, it doesn't matter.

Eryngium – he's standing a few feet away.
She turns to look at him, blows a stream
of smoke at the sky and stubs out the cig.
Sea holly, he says, *eryngium maritimum*.

Evie gets up, gives a small nod, mumbles,
Thanks, and walks towards the water.

                    *

He turns up on the beach now and then,
tells her the names of plants, talks about
seaweed and salt water. Evie barely answers.

Months might pass without him appearing –
when he does he continues as if
he's never been away.
                    When he speaks
his voice is educated – *Boring,* Evie thinks.
Like a solicitor, or that Social Services
manager that tried to get Mam in court.
No accent to place him anywhere,
not distinct, nothing definitive,
a hint of her own flat vowels, odd figures
of speech you could hear in the Co-op
when old people talked amongst themselves.
And something, somewhere else, behind it,
an occasional rise that could be a question.
She senses those inflections are one's
he'd choose to keep quiet if he could,
that in talking about a skate's egg-case
or the great mats of miniature succulents,
he forgets himself and a few escape.

Some years he's there a lot, sometimes
she doesn't see him through summer and autumn
then he'll show up in sleety winter squalls.

Stacking shelves or pricing biscuits,
Evie runs through the lists in her head

of plants and birds he's told her about –
common names first, then proper names

> *before all this started I didn't think there was anything that could*
> *stop   start   carry on the same   nothing nice at least*

> *I still don't trust it*

> *but the names are quiet things*

> *lists are quiet things*

*

He points out a great, green clump
with elegant polished leaves – she picks one
holds it towards him. *Sea-beet- eat it,*
she directs.
          Don't pick where dogs piss,
he reminds her. She lifts the leaf
to her lips, laughs at his appalled
expression.
          Evie knows he wants
something – not sex, she's sure of that.
They walk Black Tower Lane, wander down
towards the South end. She asks about
the bare clay of the beach and the layers
of sand in the unstable banks smashed by
winter weather and the slam of spring tides,
when onshore winds hurl water's huge weight
relentlessly at the stunned shore.
He tells her of glaciers grinding out rock
as they crept South, how they carrying the clay
that made the thin strip of the island –
of long-shore drift, of sediment and stone

washing in, washing out – water and wind
making the land – taking the land.

He asks what she thinks about him turning up,
she shrugs. Does she wanted to ask
anything about him, she snorts,
gives him the fuck-you face she'd perfected
standing outside some head's office, waiting
to be told again she was wasting her chance
to make something of herself – her life.

The sun's getting hotter, the beach beneath
her bare feet blistering. For three days
the tide has flooded with barely a wave,
sea swelling as though the bay is skin
and water is oozing through pores
without worrying sand – *like water and air
are the same thing* – Evie thinks. She slips
her toes back in battered trainers,
scuffs to the water's edge, kicks each one
away from the tide-line and walks in
until only her head is out of the water,
then that too sinks.
                        She breaks the surface
further out, rolls forward, flicks her feet
over her head in a showy silver arc.
The Watcher on the shore smiles.

When the snub black nose of a seal
appears, he stands to see. There's two –
their intent, curious faces turned
to the girl. They track her swim
along the beach. The big male dives,
surfaces a few metres from Evie.
She stops. The seal stops too, hangs

in the water, so close she can clearly see
each whisker, the 'W' of its nostrils,
the orb of wide-sets eye in a skull
like a beach boulder. It rolls over
and sinks from sight. Evie follows –
for a few seconds she can see flippers
then two faces turn back to hers
and they're gone.
                    When she gets out
he's reading – she glares, picks up her pile
of things and hoiks them away. As soon as
she's dry enough she lights a cig,
wanders back to The Watcher. The book is open –
one page jam-packed with jittering letters
that make her feel queasy, the opposite one
a picture – *rest harrow, Ononis repens,*
she says and flicks the book down the beach.

*

When Mam catches Covid mid-March
that first frightening year of the pandemic
she gets very sick but still won't go
to hospital. Evie can see the horror
in her face as she fights for each breath.
begs for a cig to help her breathe.
When she wheezes, *I'm drowning Evie,*
Evie rings 999.
Seeing paramedics with Mam's skinny body
is like watching a black and white film with the sound
turned down, on a screen at the end of a tunnel.

All she could remember afterwards
was the sense of Mam getting smaller, more distant,
and how powerless she was to stop it happening,

how pathetically feeble her hands and arms were
when she'd tried to hold Mam's shoulders up
in the hours till the ambulance crew arrived.

Mam's months in Intensive Care
are terrible for Evie. Then wonderful too.
Worry wakes her constantly at night.
She phones the ward shaking with panic
to be told every time, *No change,* by a nurse
whose voice is verging on exhaustion and anger.

Twice in the early hours she leaves home,
walks to the hospital. Security won't
allow her in, say she'd be arrested
for breaking curfew if she doesn't clear off.
This second time she walks and walks –
over Quarry Brow to the slag-banks,
across the black bridge, past the school –
not back to the flat, she can't be there –
along the track at the top of the beach –
a fence, a gate, ground rising gently.
She knows this place, the sudden edge,
the lip of over-hanging land,
the drop down to the shore. She stops,
scared there'll be nothing there if she takes
another step.

       Light has been leaking
over the sub sheds on the far channel side
since she reached the cinder path.
Now the sun's up she starts to make out
land from air, sea from sky.
She shuffles back from the drop, sits down
on the sheep cropped turf. Her hand slips
to her right pocket without her realising –

if every shop in the world wasn't shut
to try to stop the virus spreading
she'd have gone to the nearest garage, bought cigs.
Since she stopped smoking the week Mam got ill
she hadn't wanted a smoke – she did now.

Out to the West the offshore wind-farm
is visible, though vague, near the hazy horizon.
There's barely a breeze but suddenly Evie
thinks of huge tides, of onshore winds,
waves biting into the cliff's soft sand,
and moves back a bit more.
      The Watcher
had told her the island was wider once,
stretched out to sea a mile further at least,
pointed out the petrified forest far off
in the bay. She thinks the place back
a thousand. ten thousand, a million years –
sees the land rising, sea shrinking, a river
of ice flowing forward – swallowing – receding –
sees herds of wildebeest crossing savannahs –
mountains ranges rising – eroding.

A vast flock of knot lift off, fly low
in a dark streaming cloud, suddenly white
with each sharp swerve.
      High above a speck
circles nearer– a bird – is swooping and soaring
then Amelia Goose, the giggling bad girl
who lives in a blue house with wings but no door
on a rock in the ocean – Amelia Goose,
who whispered and chanted, who didn't care
and who never got scared, who flew with her old Gran
hunting for fishermen, hungry for flesh –
Amelia Goose is gloriously there –

her huge white wings filling the world –
Get gone Evie, get gone, get gone,
Amelia hollers, unravelling herself.

    Not chicken nuggets   Amelia Goose only eats raw flesh

Mam had been good about Amelia,
let Evie talk to her when they went shopping,
made room on the sofa so she could watch telly,
didn't make a fuss when they had to wait for her,
but she went wild when Evie said that –
Amelia Goose only eats raw flesh –
her face stared in shock, her hand flew out,
printed four fingers on Evie's bare leg.

Amelia's gone again and Mam's wired up
to breathing machines, being washed and moved
about by people she doesn't know
and wouldn't want touching her. Evie winces.

The heavy coconut scent is starting
to lift off the spikes of sun-warmed gorse
when she gets up and slowly makes her way home.

    *

Mam's benefits are still being paid,
she should ring the social worker. She doesn't.

In those weeks when Mam isn't there
Evie feels something shift – a thought thing –
an animal thing – she can't tell but
a still, small point of calm in the chaos
starts to settle, as if molecules of silence,
the absence of another's needs,

the smell of the food she's started to cook,
the coffee table cleared of clutter,
are all beginning to accrete,
each attracted to the gravitational tug
of the others. The first time she's aware
of it is when she's sitting in bed
with the curtains wide open, watching thick,
gray, cumulous clouds glide
past the opening light and her pulse
slows slightly, her chest walls seem
to expand and air fills every part of her.
When she breaths out, her whole body –
feet, shoulders, face – sag and sink
deeper down into the matrass
and the bed, the room, the house – are sea

> when the lasses at work go for a night out they always ask me
> most of them are older than I am   they're alright   sometimes I
> go   they like a drink   they tried to get me to drink at first but
> I'm not touching that stuff   they usually end up at The Nines or
> Cav's for a dance   that's the best part   them dancing   some
> of them are good   Sandra off the checkout starts with the others
> wiggling and giggling   after a while some kind of switch seems
> to flick over in her and she's dancing by herself   for herself
> lost in it   the lasses stand back and cheer when she does it   I
> love it   I've seen this look flit over her face when it happens   I
> couldn't make it out for a while then I recognised it   a kind of mix
> mostly fear and then that moment when you start to come and you
> lose yourself   it's how I feel in the sea   Sandra dancing is
> like seeing myself in the sea   I never felt anything like it anywhere
> else until I watched those clouds through the window when Mam was
> in hospital and the sea was there inside me   The Watcher asked
> me if I was ever lonely   am I lonely   seeing Sandra dance is the
> only time I think I even know what loneliness is

While Mam is in ICU Evie's days
begin to find form, learn a rhythm
she knows she has to keep if she
is going to manage when Mam gets home.

When Mam doesn't die and doctors decide
to take her off life support, see what happens,
Evie rings them repeatedly, refusing
to give consent, sometimes screaming,
sometimes begging, finally threatening them.
They block her phone number, tell security
to make sure she doesn't get in. Then they do it.

When they ring to tell Evie her mother
was breathing by herself ... *holding her own ...
body fighting back ... too early to tell ...*
she could hear the doctor's disbelief.
She couldn't speak. The voice continues –
oxygen levels ... concern over cardiac ...
Her brain is absorbing bits of what
he's saying but her mouth won't work.
hello ... hello ... are you still there?
Evie hears exhaustion in
the stranger's voice – every syllable
seems dragged down by his helplessness.
Thank you. Evie's two words are weirdly
formal and stilted but she has no way
to say – *here is my heart – here –
take it – here is my thankfulness –
my sweetest, greatest gratitude
for what you've done. Thank you.*

She shakes as she puts the phone down –
a thousand people a day are dying,
most of them much healthier than Mam

but Mam's alive and breathing by herself.

They said she'd need rehab, her lungs
and heart had taken a hammering,
her walking and balance were both bad,
her memory, hearing, eye-sight shot,
she was severely underweight.
Mam did exactly what Evie expected –
at three am, two days after
she was transferred to a general ward,
a taxi pulls up, Evie pays the driver
and holds Mam up as she hobbles in.
No luggage? she says and Mam laughs,
a croaking, grating kind of cackle,
and crumples onto the closest chair.
Get me a fag for fuck's sake Evie.
You've stopped smoking, Evie says,
and as for drink, we'll talk about that
tomorrow. Eat this. She hands Mam
a bowl with a few Rice Krispies in the bottom
floating in milk. Mam eats them.

*

Their ground floor flat is on the island –
Mam preferred town but she hadn't argued.
Evie is shocked by how much Mam
doesn't argue and strangely saddened
by the loss of the irrational, impulsive woman
who told teachers to fuck off when
they complained Evie was causing trouble,
who'd tell the Social anything and get away
with most of it, who more than once danced
Evie round and round when they got
an urgent needs payment, who could pack

everything they owned in three bin bags
and a couple of carriers and cart the lot
to their next place and never burst one.

Evie has hold of their money now,
pays the bills, buys what they need.
Every day she expects Mam
to kick off, demand a drink, a cig,
her benefits back. But she doesn't.
At first she won't eat Evie's food,
asks for cornflakes, cream-crackers and jam,
Evie ignores her.

*

She hasn't swum
since Mam got sick more than two years ago.
Her days are quiet, work had been
OK about her being off after
the shop reopened. She'd expected the sack
or at least a fuss and a lot of hassle
but the manager had told her to get the doctor
to sign her off for the next six months.
When she's due back, he rings her up,
asks how things are, what she wants to do,
says he didn't want to interfere, says she
could apply for carer's allowance,
says Mam should probably be getting PIP.
Evie hears her voice grow louder,
faster, more shrill, she's shouting –
Mam isn't disabled and she isn't
a fucking nurse – they didn't need PIP
she wasn't going to fill in forms,
tell some stranger if Mam could wipe
her own arse – if he wanted to sack her,

he should just do it. When she stopped
he asked, *Do you want your old hours back?*
Yes, she says and hangs up on him.

*

Tea's in the oven, I'm going out for a bit –
Mam's magazine falls to the floor,
her forehead creases, shoulders hunch –
only a quick swim. I'll be OK, Evie says.
Mam's scared, *I knew you'd go sooner or later.*
It's like me and drink, you have to have it.
Evie tries to keep herself calm,
but the shock of hearing Mam say, *drink,*
forces hands into fists, her throat to tighten,
panic rockets her heart rate too high,
her breathing too shallow and far too fast –
Don't you dare even think about drink,
we're not going back now, I couldn't cope.
There's a buzzing in her brain,
a shrill, relentless sound, a shriek –
sound it out   sound it out   sound it out   sound it out
She can't make it stop – mind becomes mist –
sound it out   sound it out   sound it out   sound it out
sound it out   sound it out   sound it out   sound it out
She sways, grabs the sofa for support.
Mam stretches as if she could catch her,
the sleeve of her cardi shakes with the effort
of holding her thin arm high in the air.
I won't, I promise. I don't ever want
to go back to that. I'll behave myself Evie.
Evie slumps on the sofa, her head
in Mam's lap. *Oh, Mam.... look at us!*
Mam bends over her, kisses her hair –
Cross my heart and hope to die babe.

Late autumn air – almost high tide
yet the sea is smooth, water floods quietly.
She's grateful for its gentle welcome,
its slow breathing out, breathing in –
when she sinks her body under
the cold of it is clear, singing pain –
skin   synapse   sense   thought

become balance

                    holding

                                  being held

                    *

The snowdrops she planted three years ago
have come up. Not a sign of life, then this –
a scatter of tiny, pale spears. Evie squats,
smooths dead grass back to see them better –
stalks so slender she daren't breathe on them
for fear she'll break them with her breath-weight.
And flowers – three perfect, pure white petals,
the shape of them so exquisitely elegant
as they loosen their lovely embrace
on three smaller heart shaped lobes inside –
at once all the pity and love and aloneness
of the two of them, her and Mam,
their little lives, are almost too much.
And immediately comes the thought of cold –
of salt and the lift and sway of the tide –
the kindness of water – it's kiss on her body –
its endlessness.

                    She'd only ever
cut the coarse grass at the back of the flat.
As food got more scarce she planted potatoes,
grew peas and greens – never flowers
until she saw the bags of bulbs
on sale in B&Q. Now snowdrops
grow in their garden. She thinks of The Watcher,
his knowledge of plants, of the way the earth worked,
his tenderness when he touched a leaf.
She hadn't let him see she was pleased
when he showed up, maybe that was why
he'd stopped. The last time was when the pandemic
was only a new sort of flu somewhere else.
They'd sat in the dunes with the dark pools behind them,
looked out on the bay at the incoming tide
and he'd talked of infection, a terrible sickness
that was going to happen across the world soon.
He glanced sideways at her then back to the beach,
she remembered quite clearly his look of concern –
Be very careful, this virus is a killer –
then he'd touched the back of her hand for a moment.
And those who are already frail will die first.

Perhaps he was one of the hundreds of thousands
who'd died in the decade from waves of infection
since the sickness was let loose to rip through the land.
The numbers still haunt her – so many dead!
The image she sees is always the same one –
a mountain of bodies all waxy and lifeless,
their limbs hanging limp, their dead faces filled
with sorrow – they turn to her, lips mouthing words
she can't understand.

              We've got snowdrops, she says.
Snowdrops? Mam asks. *Are you sure it's not weeds?*

Taking the mug of tea from Mam's fingers,
she slides her arms under shoulders and thighs,
scoops Mam up off the sofa in one move.
Mam's laughing loudly, as Evie lifts her
she grabs her neck. Outside in the garden
the white winter shimmer of sun makes her squint,
What are you going to do, you daft bugger?
Put me down. Evie pretends to drop her.
Mam shrieks as Evie sits her on a heap
of blankets topped by the spare duvet,
throws an old tartan rug in her lap.
For fuck's sake Evie, the grass'll be soaking.
Evie tuts, *I've put bin bags down,*
stop whingeing and have a look at my snowdrops.
Mam gazes at dead grass – *Where?*
Evie tuts again, sweeps her arms
as if the back garden were the great estate
of some mansion. *Everywhere,* she says.
And then Mam sees them. Slowly her hand
lifts from the blanket – she draws breath
breathes out her hushed amazement – one sound.
One letter, Evie thinks – *the letter O.*

Like free bloody birds. Mam's looking up
at the bare branches of next door's cherry tree.
I read that at school – Like free bloody birds.
The back garden is warmed by a winter sun
raking through bare branches. Mam tilts
her face to it, keeps eyes closed,
It's part of a poem ... I used to love reading ...
she turns to her daughter, *I didn't mean ...*
Evie stands. *I'll go and get*
your shoes – and don't try to stand up
on your own, you'll end up on your arse.

*

The year had been mild – misty and wet
but the storms that struck again and again
that winter were the worst they'd known.

Mam's on her mobile, scrolling and swiping,
*I'll help you learn ... look at this,
I found it on the internet, it's
about reading. I mean not reading ...*
Evie keeps watching TV. *Waste of time.*
I. Can't. Read. Remember?
Mam chews the inside of her cheek
Stop it, Evie snaps. *You'll give yourself
an ulcer.*
        Always fucking right, aren't you!
Evie's stares, mouth slightly open
in surprise – Mam never gets mad now –
*It's not just you, you know, there's thousands
of people that can't read or write –
it's got a name –*
        *I know all the names
for it,* Evie snaps. *Shall I go over some?
There's 'thicko' and 'stupid' and 'brainless.' Oh,
and 'moron.' Then there's 'loser.' And 'cretin' –
that a bit special – different, don't you think?*
Mam blows out slowly. *I'm trying to help –
it's called dyslexia and we can do
something about it –* Evie changes channels.
Mam keeps going – *We could try, couldn't we?
It's not your brain – well it is in a way.*
Evie laughs loudly, *Thanks for that!*
Turn the telly off, Mam tells her.
*There's this thing – Toe by Toe, it's called
then there's Snappy Lessons and another one ...*

Evie turns to her. *If you think I'm going
to do something called Snappy Lessons
you can think again – I'm nearly thirty –
it won't be snappy – and it won't work.*
Mam scrabbles at the side of the sofa,
*You're not – you're doing Toe by Toe,
I've bought the book off eBay. Ten minutes
a day and even a cretin can learn
to read. Go get a pencil girl.*

*

Learning to read hadn't been half as hard
with Mam as it was at school – the way
Mam taught her, with that book she bought
and her patience and taking the piss now and then
made it more normal.

     Evie finishes the book
she'd got in a charity shop, when shops were still open –
'Klara and the Sun.' She thinks of memories
overlapping, Manager not looking that one last time.
And in her head she hears herself saying,
rest harrow, Ononis repens, sees The Watcher
turn away when the book flies from his hands.

Radio's more reliable for finding out
what's happening – some main-stream –
more often people putting out what info
they could since the government cut internet access
to an hour here and there. The analogue set
Evie salvaged from an empty flat
was a life-line, at least when the power came on.

Reports are alarming – world weather gone haywire,

winds of a hundred miles an hour,
storm surges and floods more frequent. Today
the weather forecast says warm and misty
for forty-eight hours, followed by heavy rain.

> *we should leave*
> *how weird that she won't go*
> *she never liked the island   said there was too much sea   last*
> *year was bad she'll die if the heating keeps going off this winter*
> *what if they stop bringing food over   if the water pipes burst*
> *again we've had it there's not many left just the ones in the*
> *community centre us few here and the camp up at Thirteen Corners*

Evie gets her coat and goes out.
There were warnings the bridge was too weak to cross,
no-one was to try – they should wait for the boat.
But the boat hasn't been. The tarmac on the bridge
has gone in places, its iron parapets
corroded and full of holes as Evie
makes her way up the middle. Half way across
her foot forces the crumbling surface
to give way. She steps back in shock,
sees the swirling tide through the hole
she's made – the speed of it scares her –
greedy, churning water that wants
to swallow the girders, swallow her.
Here, where the bridge used to lift to let
sail pass, the painted parapet
becomes railing – rotting now since the sea
has risen so far that for hours some days
the bridge is submerged, the only parts showing,
the top of the lift house and the abutments.
The wind is wilder than she'd expected,
it snatches at Evie, unbalances her briefly.
Mam needs new inhalers, nobody's going

to bring them, she knows she's got to get
across today – the med vans only visit
once a week and there's no other way
to get what you need since the government
did what they described as "restructuring
health provision." She pushes on –
if she can see someone, collect Mam's meds
before the tide turns, she might be back
today. If not, she'll be there all night.

The vans will be parked up at the old Asda's –
in low-lying places, the road is permanently
underwater. Raised wooden walkways
have been built so people can still get about,
they're slippery though, treacherous for someone
not good on their feet. Evie's glad –
maybe there won't be too many there,
maybe she'll make it back over the bridge.

She looks about for a stick or something
to support her but there's nothing near,
just the piles of tattered plastic
that litter high-water lines. It's impossible
to make any speed. Approaching Asda
she sees the milling mass – crowds converging,
volunteers in Hi-Viz vests
are funnelling people in different directions,
ensuring distancing laws are enforced,
security guards with guns on show
patrol entrances and exits to the perimeter,
making sure everyone's masks are on,
checking ID, scanning irises,
their own made invisible by mirrored visors.

The queues creep forward. Evie's feet

are soaking, her only shoes squelching
with each slow step – cold is stealing
into her bones – she won't make it back
over the bridge today, that's certain.

The fuggy heat of the van wraps round her.
Condensation collects as wet bodies warm,
runs down walls and windows in spite
of the huge extractor fans. Evie's eyes
ache with tiredness – all she wants
is to sit down. There's been no seats
in public places since the second pandemic.
She's dizzy – if she faints, she'll lose
her place – the smell of the sanitization
vapour hangs heavy – she mustn't vomit –
the air is viscous, Mr Ferguson's voice
is telling her to sound it out.
You can fuck right off Mr Ferguson.
Had she thought it? Said it aloud?
How loud? Security are looking over –
She raises the folded piece of paper
she's holding – *sorry   sorry   I thought
I'd lost it   my list   here it is   sorry.*

Mam'll be worried, though Evie had warned
she might not be back before the tide turned.

In one way, Mam's walking being so bad
was a blessing, she couldn't stand for long
without Evie so at least she wouldn't
be wandering about. She had food, a flask,
the phone for emergencies only. Power cuts
came with no notice, dragged on for days
one winter they went on for over three weeks.

There was a time when Evie knew
Mam's worrying was because she needed
Evie to keep her safe – from herself
more than anything. That had altered –
how it happened, she couldn't say
but Mam's 'I'– the helpless, hopeless
'me' of her had all but gone –
these days they were easy together.

Evie has hidden the inhalers inside
her coat. She's not scared but she's cautious –
most folk are fine but there's always a few
who aren't on any official records,
who take their chances where they can.
There's nothing for them on the island,
here it's different. A woman is watching her,
a child clinging onto to her leg.
She pretends not to have noticed them,
walks through the gate towards town.
The wind's got up – great gusts across
Ramsden Square whip dead grass
into thrashing thoughts, plastic bags
into dancing, diving kites. A man
hunkered down in a doorway weighs her up,
she forces her feet to walk steadily,
turns down a side-street towards the channel.

A couple appear so suddenly, she gasps –
You alright love? the young woman asks.
They're not wearing masks. Evie moves back.
Yes...yes...I'm good...thanks.
They stand side by side – she can't tell
if they blocking the pavement on purpose –
the terraced houses seem to shuffle closer –
she looks the man in the eye. *Excuse me,*

she says, holding his gaze – he smiles
and steps aside.
                    Even then Evie
isn't sure what they want – maybe she misjudged
the situation? Maybe they were trying
to help? She hurries between them
holding her breath but forcing herself
to nod in passing. Something plastic and light
bounces on the pavement behind her.
The couple have stopped – she stops –
You dropped this love. He's holding a blue
inhaler out – fear freezes Evie –
she clutches her coat round her chest –
It's alright, we won't do anything –
I'll put it here, you can pick it up.
he says. They back off – Evie edges
forwards – eyes still firmly fixed
as they turn around and walk away.
She grabs the inhaler, watches them go –
Thank you, she shouts. They wave as they
turn the corner.
                    Town is less safe
for Evie – she needs to find somewhere
to spend the hours until she can cross
the bridge, get back to the island. Trying
in the dark would be stupid, waiting it out
over two tides is the only way.
Even at low water Evie won't swim
the channel – sewage has gone straight in
since the treatment plant flooded five years ago
and there's dangerous debris – bits of old boats,
plastic panelling, timber, the steel
frameworks from closed channel-side factories
are trapped in mud or tossed like litter
to slam into banks and batter the bridge

in the relentless rampage of the sea.

She'd never been scared of it – all her life
the sea had been sanctuary. But that was before
storms grew stronger, ate away land,
and increasing high tides inundated their island.

There's an overgrown area that's almost always
out of water – the old channel-side park –
with bramble and bushes she can hide in
if there's anyone around. And if it floods
there's a small stand of trees at the top.
Her feet are wet but the early autumn air
is warmer than it was this morning
and the sun hasn't yet lost its day heat.
She pushes into the patch of shrubbery
on the hill, finds herself in a open space
about four metres across, in the sun
and out of the wind. It doesn't look like
anyone's been near – there'll be ticks about–
ants and spiders as well but insects
don't bother Evie. She tugs her shoes
and socks off, hangs them in the sun,
takes her water bottle and bit of bread
from her pocket. All she can see
is grass, sky and the bramble bush walls
of her home for the night. There are noises nearby –
not people – some creature – a cat perhaps?
Cats on their own didn't cause much trouble
though tales of cat colonies were going round school
when Evie was little – the cat woman who lived
down the derelict mill site in an old van
with her hundreds of cats she let shit
wherever they wanted – some of the big kids
said she let them shit in her hair.

One boy reckoned he'd seen her through
the tall metal fence – *totally naked* –
I could see everything, he said. She was the one
who sent her cats out to roam round town,
climbing in cots, crawling in children's beds,
covering faces, smothering sleepers.
Dogs were a problem since the first pandemic
when people got puppies to please their children
in the long years of the lockdown,
then threw them out when they went back to work.

Whatever it is in the undergrowth is small –
a snuffling, flustered sort of thing –
not a rat then, rats don't furtle about
like this thing, rats are smart – a robin
flusters from the bush, a fat pale grub
clamped in its beak. It considers Evie
with one furious black eye and flaps off.

She checks the inhalers, lies back and looks up
at the circle of sky with the sun slipping west.
The air has a heavy, fruity smell –
woodsmoke from the fires the few families
were lighting for cooking and warmth
since power cuts got bad – black-berries
ripening round Thirteen Corners Lane –
leaf litter mouldering – *Composure,*
Evie thinks, *being calm and in control.*

Once she got going Evie had fallen
deeply in love with the old dictionary
she got in a charity shop when words
started to make sense. She loved losing herself
in it, opening it to look up one word,
being distracted by another,

then another and another.
When she emerged the room seemed suddenly
strange – proportions and perspectives
not quite right – a woozy Wonderland –
then she'd blink and it all slid back.

It's cool but not cold. The moon comes up
over the sub-sheds – three quarters there.
You could see the night sky clearly now
since street lights were switched off, factories shut.
Stars look still, like the ones they'd hung
on lengths of cotton for the school Christmas play –
she knows they're not – they're spiralling – or maybe
they are still, and it's her that's spinning?
Weariness weighs her limbs and eyes –
the noiseless night draws her down
into warm earth until the world closes.

Evie   *Evie*
                        Evie is walking
through swaying grass, so tall she can't
see where she's going – someone's shouting –
Evie   *Evie*
                        And Amelia Goose –
dear, dear Amelia Goose
is swooping and laughing, soaring and yelling,
coming closer until her wonderful white wings
are almost touching Evie – air
swirls faster, she can barely stand,
now pushing, now lifting her high off the ground –
she's looking for Amelia – listening
for Amelia but the wild wings
have stopped their fantastic flapping,
no-one is calling her name,
there's nothing and nobody holding her

and she's howling as she hurtles to earth.

As soon as she opens the door she can tell
someone's been in the house. Mam's sitting
on the sofa, the usual scatter of her things –
note-pad, pens, nail file, flask,
hair-brush, books are all there, but different –
odd – *Orderly,* Evie thinks.
Sit down, Mam says

> *I couldn't make head or tail of what she was saying   telling me
> things that seemed to come from different worlds and in a weird
> order   she was crying but not making any sound   crying so
> much the front of her jumper was soaked then she stopped and turned
> to me and looked at my face as if she was trying to find something
> and when her eyes looked directly into mine I didn't know her   I
> was looking at a stranger then myself then Mam then someone else I
> thought I knew but I didn't know them*

She'll come back Evie, I think she'll come back.
Evie tucks the blanket round Mam.
Let's hope so, eh.

*

Evie knows knocking out the old fireplace
is the only way they'll stay warm and be able
to cook now the power supply looked like it was
going to go off for good sometime soon –
the chimney stack would need sorting as well.
She's prowling round picking up anything
she can use to break through brickwork.
*Why don't you wait? Jess'll be back,
she'll help you,* Mam says. But it's been
four weeks and Evie's worried about winter.

It was easy at first – the opening only
covered by plasterboard. In a couple of hours
she's made a huge, soot smeared hole
in the chimney breast. She's left Mam in bed
out of the dust. There's a cold draft –
what if she makes it worse? The notes she wrote
when they still had wi-fi say, 'Check chimney
is clear.' The dried grass takes time to light,
she bends over glowing stalks, blows gently.
Flames flicker then crackle – smoke
billows back in her eyes – she can't see,
can't stop coughing – crawls away blindly,
finds the front door and opens it wide.
When the flames die down and the air in the room
is clear enough she checks on Mam,
breathes a sigh of relief to see she's still asleep.

*There's a bit of smoke from the chimney. It could
be blocked?* The woman in the doorway is a stranger.
Like Mam? – No, not like Mam, Evie thinks,
and a part of her is pleased. But she is –
she is like Mam – shoulders stronger,
different hair – not like hers
and Mams – she's taller too – her mouth
and nose aren't theirs   but her eyes...
and something about the way she stands
weight to one side... something about
the slight sideways tilt of her head...
about the way she walks, is like Mam.

Jessica. Evie says the name slowly
as if trying out its shape on her tongue,
hearing what her own voice made
of the word for the woman who is her twin.

*It might be blocked ... I don't know much
about chimneys ...* She's anxious, shifts her weight
from one foot to the other. Evie frowns,
*You shouted my name – the night in the park
when I couldn't get back over the bridge –
I heard you – you were shouting my name.*
The woman glances away, her gaze
moves to Pot Dog on the mantlepiece –
I thought if....

        I thought I might ...

*I found the flat – you'd gone to get
the inhalers – she was scared in case
something bad had happened to you.*

How did you get here? Evie asks.
*By boat – a boat with a motor ... a motorboat
I suppose you'd call it ...*
        Evie shakes her head,
*the flat I mean, how did you find it,
find us?*
        *Dad said he thought you'd stay
on the island ... that you would always want
to be near the sea. He said you used
to live on a road called Ramsgate Crescent
not far from the bridge. So I got the boat ...*
Evie's confused. *He's dead, isn't he?*
Jess shuts her eyes, nods silently.
He used to talk about you both ... this island ...

*Shall we check the chimney out,
see if there's something stuck in it?*

        *

That first winter the two of them
collect drift-wood to feed the fire
in the hearth they'd made. Mam's breathing is bad
but she's comfortable – content – happy to have
her twins together. Evie had expected
it to be difficult – it isn't – there's intimacy
in days as the two work and talk together,
in nights sitting with Mam while the fire
dwindles in the grate. In those gentling hours
Evie sees Sandra dancing – The Watcher
crouching over a clump of sea kale –
Mr Ferguson's mouth moving
and moving but making no noise – gray waves –
a great bird gliding above the dunes –
salt drying to stars on her skin.

Jess tells her sister what she knows of where
their father was from – his stories of life
with a grandmother sent to Australia –
a home child – a migrant made to work
on an outback farm – the things she told him
of cold, rolling waves and seabirds calling,
and her family back in the time before
they took her away across the world.
Evie has nothing, no history to offer,
and Jess doesn't ask.

*

The cherry blossom is even more beautiful
this spring– as if all the softness in the world,
every tender thought, had been wrapped in pink petals
and festooned in ridiculous frilly bundles
to its branches, before leaves even got going.
When wind flusters in off the sea,

pink dots dance circles in the air,
drift down to earth. Evie knows now
this will be the last spring, their last year –
she'd told herself there'd be more time,
other seasons, maybe one more spring.

Mam's drowsy but she wants to keep talking –
to tell Evie things that had happened
but never says anything about her own past.
Evie lets Mam speak, listens silently,
holds her hand till she drifts into sleep.

*

We'll have to go soon. Her sister touches
Evie's arm as she speaks. Evie nods,
*She wants to see the snowdrops again –
can we wait a bit longer, it's still winter Jess?*
Jess shakes her head. *We've left it late.
The boys have been watching weather patterns,
when they get radio reception. They reckon
we can make it but we must leave soon.
They'll bring the boat as close as they can,
we have to work out how to get Mam there
without hurting her.*
            Hearing someone say, *Mam*
had angered Evie until she understood
that Jess was using the name Evie used,
not attempting to make any kind of claim.

She'd never thought of Mam as anything
other than Mam – not 'Christine' and certainly
not 'Chrissy.' Jess told her twin what she knew
of their birth and what happened to the two of them,
said their father always called Mam 'Chrissy,'

talked about her a lot before he died.

The photos too, astonished Evie –
Jess and a small, smiling boy at a fun fair,
another of them in an outdoor pool,
one of those old-fashioned lido ones –
Charlie, she said. The same boy but older,
with another lad, standing by a tent,
both squinting into the sun – *That's Sam.*
They've been best friends since they started school.
More snaps – the boys on mountain-bikes,
on a night out, lying by a lake
their upturned canoes nearby – some of Jess –
school photo, birthday party, graduation day pic –
a few of them with The Watcher – the way
he's looking at them is the same way she'd seen him
look at her once when she'd suddenly turned round.

Then this – this one image – two long lines of dancers
in checked shirts and Stetsons and cowboy boots caught
mid step, left thumbs hooked through broad leather belts,
right arms reaching back as if
the dancers were riders, ready to slap
the rump of horse. And in the front row,
Mam laughing, face turned to the man
dancing beside her, and him grinning back,
the two of them impossibly young.
She came here to teach line dance, Jess says,
at the hotel where Dad worked – he loved it
from the start – loved her – he wasn't
bad Evie – after we were born
I think it was too much – they were kids –
piss poor, no home, no help. He never
stopped thinking about you both. He wasn't
a bad man.

Evie nods, *I know.*

Jess being there, being so easy,
helping her look after Mam – and Mam
letting herself loosen into their care –
her and Jess fitting the fragments
of each other's lives into their own,
was a sort of sloughing off for Evie –
*as if I'm starting to live in a skin
that finally fits,* she says to her twin.

*

They've taken the kitchen door down,
made handles to help them carry it,
straps to keep Mam safe. It stands
beside the back door for the four of them
to bring her down to the boat.

Are you sad?
Mam asks. *You've never not lived by the sea,
from when you were small it seemed to be
in your blood. It'll be hard for you.*
Evie looks up from packing Mam's medicines,
Not sad exactly – and in her mind's eye,
a patch of brilliant moss, so bright
that the bleached grass and bare brambles
enclosing it seem lit – she's staring
open-mouthed at a colour too shocking,
too vividly green to belong in the dunes,
in the dead days of winter. The Watcher is there,
Listen, he says. And the sea rolls in.

It was the last time Evie ever saw him.
I don't think I know how I feel if I'm honest.

She lowers the lid, snaps the bag shut.
*And anyway, if it is in my blood
it'll always be there wherever I am.
What about you, you wanted to see
the snowdrops again?* She turns to mam.
There's no time now, she says.
Mam shrugs.

*

ACKNOWLEDGEMENTS

I'd like to thanks all the poets and story-tellers whose brilliant writing has made me ache with wonder and respect and the knowledge that to even get within sight of the foothills of their work will take me the rest of my life. I'm especially grateful to Thomas Hardy who turned my affection for poetry into a deep and lasting love, in two minutes in a classroom of Furness College of FE in 1989. And Elizabeth Bishop whose poem 'At the Fishhouses' showed me an ocean I'd thought about all my life but never really known. I have drawn on that poem in my own attempts at writing the sea; I hope she wouldn't mind.

I'd like to thank Molly Mather for the beautiful cover photograph and for her thoughtful consideration of my attempts to sew water.

And huge thanks to VERVE Poetry Press and Stuart Bartholemew for having taken on this poem story, even though we agreed from the start that it may well be a ridiculous thing to make. I'm grateful too for Stuart's elegant typesetting and interior layout of this book.

ALSO AVAILABLE FROM VERVEPOETRYPRESS.COM

Eighty Four:
Poems on Male Suicide, Vulnerability, Grief and Hope

With an introduction from editor Helen Calcutt

Eighty Four was originally a new anthology of poetry on the subject of male suicide in aid of CALM. Poems were donated to the collection by Andrew McMillan, Salena Godden, Anthony Anaxogorou, Katrina Naomi, Ian Patterson, Caroline Smith, Carrie Etter, Peter Raynard, Joelle Taylor, while a submissions window yielded many excellent poems on the subject from hitherto unknown poets we are thrilled to have been made aware of.

We hope this book will shed light on an issue that is cast in shadow, and which is often shrouded in secrecy and denial. If we don't talk, we don't heal and we don't change. In Eighty Four we are all talking. Are you listening?

Available in paperback:
ISBN: 978 1 912565 13 9
188 pages • 216 x 138 • 56 poems
£11.99

And on eBook:
ISBN: 978 1 912565 79 5
£7.99

ALSO AVAILABLE FROM VERVEPOETRYPRESS.COM

Where Else:
An International Hong Kong Poetry Anthology

With an introduction from editors Jennifer Wong, Jason Eng Hun Lee & Tim Tim Cheng

Featuring both established and emerging Hong Kong poets across generations and continents, this unique anthology offers a glimpse into an exciting, diverse range of voices that make up the diasporic imagination of the contemporary Hong Kong poetry community. Adopting a diasporic approach, the anthology encompasses both native Hong Kong writers as well as expatriate and mixed-race voices who were born or have lived in the city.

Incl poems from Sarah Howe, Mary Jean Chan, Kit Fan, Marilyn Chin, Eric Yip and many more!

Available in paperback:
ISBN: 978 1 913917 36 4
252 pages • 216 x 138 • 106 poems
£14.99

And on eBook:
ISBN: 978 1 913917 79 1
£9.99

ABOUT VERVE POETRY PRESS

Verve Poetry Press is a prize-winning press that focused initially on meeting a local need in Birmingham - a need for the vibrant poetry scene here in Brum to find a way to present itself to the poetry world via publication. Co-founded by Stuart Bartholomew and Amerah Saleh, it now publishes poets from all corners of the UK - poets that speak to the city's varied and energetic qualities and will contribute to its many poetic stories.

Added to this is a colourful pamphlet series, many featuring poets who have performed at our sister festival - and a poetry show series which captures the magic of longer poetry performance pieces by festival alumni such as Polarbear and Imogen Stirling.

The press has been voted Most Innovative Publisher at the Saboteur Awards, and has won the Publisher's Award for Poetry Pamphlets at the Michael Marks Awards.

Like the festival, we strive to think about poetry in inclusive ways and embrace the multiplicity of approaches towards this glorious art.

www.vervepoetrypress.com
@VervePoetryPres
mail@vervepoetrypress.com